CONTENTS

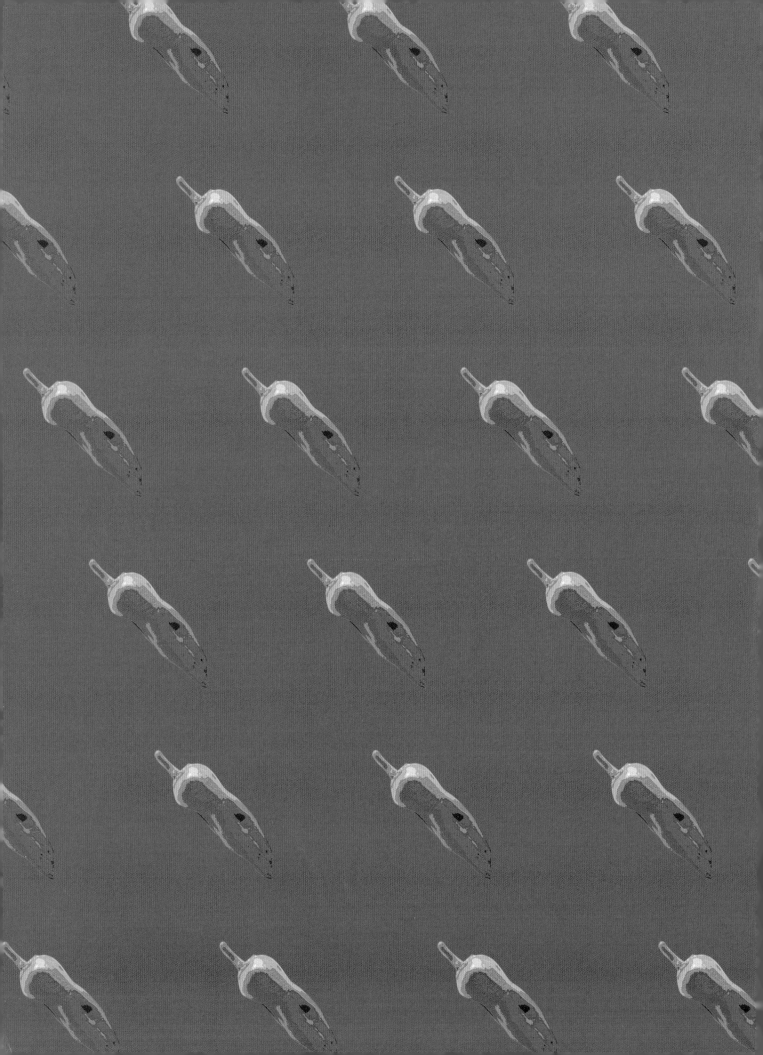

The Chilli

INTRODUCTION

Traces found indicate chillies were cultivated 8–10,000 years ago.
The first chillies were tiny wild berries grown in the Amazon jungle and from
their tiny seeds more than 150 varieties have evolved. They were grown in Mexico
and neighbouring countries as well as in the Caribbean islands.

It was the ancestors of today's Mexicans and Indians who grew chillies and it was the movement of the different tribes, hundreds of years ago, that brought about the vast array of varieties which are now available. The Spanish and Portuguese explorers took chillies on their travels and this resulted in chillies being grown along their trading routes to North and West Africa, Madagascar and India. They were quickly incorporated into the native cuisines. Around the middle of the 14th century chillies reached China, the Far East and West Indies. They even found their way to Hungary and Tibet. Today they are cultivated throughout the world but the majority are grown in Mexico, New Mexico, California, Texas, Arizona, Louisiana, Thailand and other parts of the Far East.

Whether fresh or dried, chillies are primarily associated with Mexican and Asian cuisines. They are essential in India and South-East Asia where much of the flavour and intensity of heat in the cooking is due to chillies. In China too, chilli is a popular seasoning, particularly in the Sichuan district, providing some very fiery dishes. One of the favourite Chinese sauces, Hoisin, contains this most versatile ingredient. In the past chillies were not as much liked in Europe but with the advent of more universal travel they are quickly becoming a favoured ingredient.

What are Chillies?

Chillies are related to the capsicum plant. They range from mild and sweet varieties to fiery hot that make the palate tingle and the eyes water. Their primary purpose has always been to flavour dishes but recent research suggests that they also have excellent medicinal qualities. They were one of the natural remedies used in ancient times as an expectorant, and for helping to prevent lung disorders, dissolve blood clots and kill pain. Today, this aspect is being explored in more detail.

The many different varieties come in assorted shapes, sizes, colours and names. Some are available only where they are grown and this often leads to great confusion, especially as even the spelling of the word "chilli" varies from area to area and country to country.

Cultivation of Chillies

Chillies are easy to grow in the right environment, needing only a small area and very little care and cultivation. They do best in warm, humid climates. The foliage is lush and many varieties make attractive plants, suitable for growing in pots. The berries, which develop into the fruit or chilli, have a smooth taut skin. They are hollow, consisting of fleshy membranes or veins with many seeds. The shape varies from small elongated fruits to squat, round or even square fruit which can be thin, flattened or plump. The colours range from green, red and orange to purple, brown and black, or even pale yellow or creamy white. Usually the smaller the chilli, the hotter it is but there are always the exceptions. Remember that unripe chillies are less fiery than ripe ones. As they cross-pollinate freely, unless grown separately they will breed hybrids, which can result in a hotter chilli than the original variety.

Dried Chillies and Chilli Powder

Not only are chillies available fresh, they can also be found dried, pickled and canned, as well as in chilli powder, which is probably the form that most people think of when chilli is mentioned. Oil flavoured with chillies is now available too in some food stores and delicatessens. It is mainly used for marinades and stir-fries.

Canned chillies are neither as crisp nor as fiery hot as fresh ones, whereas dried chillies can be hotter than their fresh counterparts, especially if the seeds are used as well. For heat and flavour, dried chillies and chilli powder are a better substitute than canned. Drying intensifies the flavour and pungency. Good chilli powder should be a deep rich colour, neither too powdery nor too dry and with a slightly lumpy consistency indicating that the natural oils have not

Red and yellow chillies hanging in a market in Hungary.

Chillies in a fruit and vegetable market in Mexico.

Uses of Chillies

One of the main reasons for using chillies is for their flavour; they provide an excellent means of spicing a dish that would otherwise be bland and insipid. In tropical countries chillies are used with the same frequency that peppers are in the Mediterranean area and other parts of Europe. There is a widely held belief that the hotter the climate, the hotter the food. This has the effect of raising the blood temperature to that of the air temperature, thus making you feel cool. Hot fiery food also helps the sweat glands to work, a crucial function in very hot climates.

Chillies are used in all types of savoury foods, from soups, sauces, fish, meat and poultry dishes, to chutneys, pickles and dips, as well as for garnishes.

Utensils

When using either fresh or dried chillies, a pestle and mortar is an invaluable aid in the kitchen. This will enable you to pound the chillies to the correct consistency, whether a paste is required or just finely ground chillies. You can use a food processor for grinding or pounding but it is not nearly as effective. However, a food processor or liquidizer is ideal for blending soups and sauces and forming pureés.

A selection of sharp knives is essential in any kitchen, as are heavy-based pans and bowls.

How to Handle Chillies

Great care must be exercised when handling chillies as the oils in the chillies are an irritant to the skin. A pair of rubber gloves is a good investment, for the hotter the chilli, the hotter the effect can be on your skin. Always cover any cuts on your hands when using chillies, and never rub your eyes, mouth or nose after handling chillies until you have washed your hands thoroughly. If by any chance you do get some of the chilli oil on your face or in your eyes, rinse thoroughly in plenty of cold water.

Some people advocate using oil to counteract "chilli burn" and milk is reputed by some to be better than water to drink.

been lost. These oils should leave a slight stain on the fingers when rubbed and the aroma should be intense. The most commonly known chilli powders are cayenne and paprika. These are made from one type of chilli, whereas chilli seasoning is made from a variety of different chillies. There are also many different chilli sauces on the market, Tabasco and the Caribbean Hot Pepper Sauce being among the most popular and well-known.

If you wish to dry your own chillies, thread different types of fresh chilli together, rather like a string of onions, then hang near a sunny window and leave until completely dry before storing. Dried chillies and chilli powder should be stored in airtight containers, in a cool, dark place and used within 4–6 months.

But whatever the name, spelling or type, one thing is sure: chillies are an invaluable food ingredient and no cook should be without these versatile fiery little spices.

Preparation of Chillies

To peel fresh chillies, place under a preheated grill and cook for a few minutes, turning frequently until the skin has blistered and blackened. Take care, however, not to burn the flesh. You can also pierce the chilli with a skewer and hold it over a gas flame to blister, or dip it quickly in hot oil. Once the chilli skin has blistered, place in a bowl, cover with cling film and leave the chilli to cool. (You can put the chilli into a polythene bag instead.) This will take about 10 minutes. Then peel, cut in half and discard the seeds and fleshy membrane, using a spoon or small sharp knife. Avoid washing chillies as you will remove the oils and impair their flavour.

Dried chillies should be roasted and rehydrated before use. Lightly roast or dry-fry the dried chillies for a few minutes, taking care not to burn them. Cover with very hot but not boiling water and leave to soak for about 10 minutes, until softened. Drain and use as required in the recipes. The seeds and membranes can then be easily removed and discarded.

Garnishes

Chillies can make most attractive garnishes for the dishes in which they feature. With a sharp knife or scissors, a board and a bowl of cold water, chillies can easily be transformed into flowers in about 10 minutes.

Rinse the chilli lightly; then, using a small sharp knife or scissors, slit down the length of the chilli almost to the stem, give the chilli a slight turn and cut again. Repeat the turning and cutting until the chilli has been cut all the way round. Carefully remove and discard the seeds. If any of the cuts are thick, then cut again to make finer petals. Place in a bowl of cold or iced water for 5–10 minutes, or until the chilli has curled and formed flowers. Dry gently on paper towels.

Chopped or sliced chilli can also be used as a garnish, sprinkled over the finished dish, to provide colour and extra piquancy.

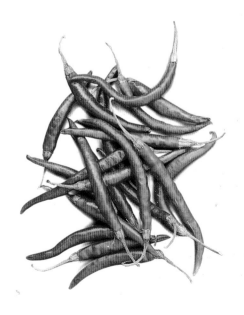

A GUIDE TO FRESH *and* DRIED CHILLIES

*Chillies are normally green in colour before ripening and
turning yellow, orange, red, purple, brown or black. They are used in
both their unripened and ripened state. Green or red is often used to describe
a different stage of ripeness rather than to denote a specific variety.
For instance, you can get a green fresno as well as a red fresno.*

*W*hen buying fresh chillies, look for firm, shiny, dry and heavy chillies, with a fresh clean aroma; avoid those that are discoloured or limp. Store, after washing and drying, wrapped in paper towels in the salad compartment of the refrigerator, where they will keep for 2–3 weeks. If chillies are kept in polythene bags, moisture will build up and spoilage will occur and if not kept in the refrigerator, they will quickly shrivel and become limp and spoil.

Remember the heat is in the membrane or vein, not the seeds, and when a recipe calls for the chilli to be deseeded, the membrane needs to be removed as well. If a hotter flavour is required than the chilli you are using will provide, simply leave the seeds and membrane intact. It is worth noting that everyone's heat tolerance varies, and what one person finds hot, another will not. Equally after eating chilli-based dishes for a time, the palate's heat tolerance builds up and it can assimilate far hotter flavours than before.

Once you have become accustomed to chillies, it is well worth experimenting by combining two or three varieties in the same dish, thus imparting a different flavour. These of course can include dried and canned chillies, chilli powders, seasonings and sauces.

Aji – *Heat 7–8 Thin-fleshed, tapering to a point, about 7.5–12.5 cm/3–5 in in length with a tropical fruit flavour and a fierce heat. Yellow, green or red in colour. Originating from Peru and other regions of South America. Ideal for salsas, sauces and pickling.*

Ají dulce – *Heat 7–8 Similar shape to a small elongated bell pepper, about 5–7.5 cm/2–3 in. in length with a fruity but hot flavour. From bright green to orange and red. Related to the Scotch bonnet and habanero. Grown in Venezuela and north-east South America. Ideal for salsas and stews.*

Amatista – *Heat 7 Wide at the stem, tapering to a point with a rounded end, about 1.25–4 cm/½–1½ in. in length. Bright purple with an earthy, sweet flavour. Grown in South America. Ideal for pickling and garnishes.*

Anaheim – *Heat 2–3 Also known as the Californian, Mexican or long green (or red) chilli. About 15 cm/6 in. in length and 5 cm/2 in in width. Either bright green or, when ripe, red. Thicker flesh than many, similar to the bell pepper with a vegetable flavour. The red Anaheim is sweeter than the green. The flavour can be improved by roasting. Grown in California, and south-west America. Dried powdered red Anaheim chillies are sold as chilli Colorado. Ideal stuffed, or for sauces and stews.*

Banana chilli – *Heat 2–3 About 15 cm/6 in. in length, pale green to light orange. Having a sweet flavour similar to a bell pepper with a thick flesh. The inside of the flesh is often rubbed with chilli powder in order to impart a stronger flavour. Grown in south-west America. Ideal for stuffing and salads.*

Chawa – *Heat 3–4 Usually curved and tapering to a point, about 7.5–12.5 cm/3–5 in. in length. Pale yellow with a thin flesh, having a sweet flavour with a hint of heat. Similar in appearance to the banana chilli. Grown on the coast of Mexico. Ideal for salads, stuffing and pickling.*

Chilli negro – *Heat 3–4 Also known as chilaca, about 15–23 cm/6–9 in. in length, and can be curved. Dark brown to almost black. Difficult to find fresh outside Mexico but any other chilli with similar heat properties or chilli powder can be substituted. The dried chilli negro is often called chilli pasilla. Grown in Mexico and parts of South America. Ideal for pickling and sauces.*

Congo – *Heat 8 A small, green, very hot chilli which turns red on ripening, about 6 mm–1.25 cm/¼–½ in. in length. Grown in the Congo, Mombasa and Zanzibar.*

De agua – *Heat 4–5 About 10–12.5 cm/4–5 in. in length, tapering to a point, and either green or red, both having a vegetable flavour similar to unripe tomatoes with a thin flesh. The red has a slightly sweeter flavour. Grown in South America. Ideal for soups, mole sauces and stuffing.*

Dutch – *Heat 6 Also known as Holland chilli, about 10 cm/4 in. in length, slightly curved and bright red. Having a hot sweet flavour with a thick flesh. The Thai chilli or red fresno can be substituted. Grown in the Netherlands. Ideal for soups, casseroles, sauces and pickling.*

Ethiopian – *Heat 2 A small chilli about 6 mm–1.25 cm/ ¼–½ in. in length. A smooth mild red chilli that is grown in Ethiopia and surrounding countries.*

Fiesta – *Heat 6–8 Ornamental chillies about 2.5–5 cm/1–2 in. in length. Related to the cayenne and Tabasco chilli, slightly tapered with a rounded end. Varying in flavour and heat from mild to hot and in colour from yellow through to red. Excellent plants for pot-growing. Grown in north Mexico and Louisiana. Ideal for garnish, salsas and stir-fries.*

Fresno – *Heat 6–7 Either green or red, about 5 cm/2 in. in length, full and plump, tapering to a round end. Has a thick flesh and is sweet and hot. Grown mainly in Mexico and California. Ideal for salsas, stuffing and sauces.*

Güero – *Heat 4–6 The generic name for any pale yellow or green chilli, can also be called blond. Can vary in size from 7.5–12.5 cm/3–5 in. Has a slightly sweet flavour with a sharp tang. Heat ranges from moderate to hot. Grown in north Mexico and the south-west of America. Ideal for yellow mole sauces and garnish.*

Guntur – *Heat 5 A deep red chilli with a compressed base about 1.25–2.5 cm/½–1 in. in length. Grown in India.*

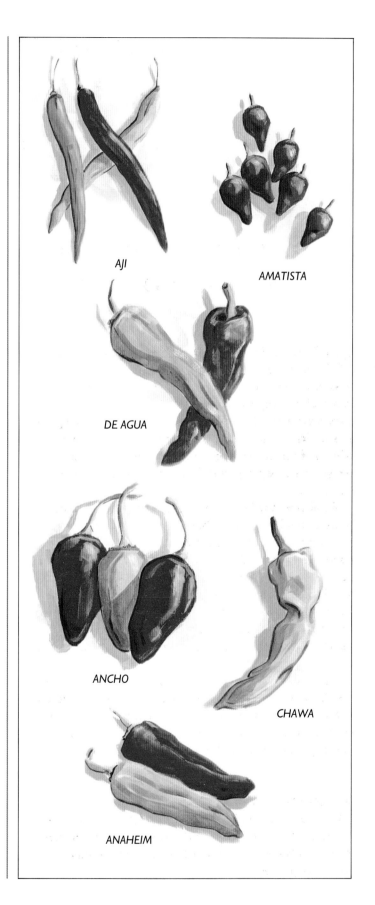

AJI

AMATISTA

DE AGUA

ANCHO

CHAWA

ANAHEIM

Habanero – *Heat 10 About 5 cm/2 in. in length with a lantern shape. Varying from green and yellow to red and reddish-purple. The ripe habanero is sweet with a tropical fruity flavour. It is one of the hottest chillies available and is closely related to the Scotch bonnet and the Jamaican hot chillies. Grown in Central America and the Caribbean. Ideal in salsas, marinades, chutneys and bottled sauces.*

Honka or Hontaka – *Heat 9 2–5 cm/¾–3 in. in length, an orange or red chilli which is wrinkled in appearance. Grown in Japan.*

Huachinango – *Heat 5–6 About 10–12.5 cm/4–5 in. in length, tapered with a rounded end. Bright red with white or pale markings on the skin. Thick-fleshed with a sweet flavour. Often smoked and dried and used to make chipotle grande. Grown in central Mexico. Ideal for salsas, casseroles and sauces.*

Hungarian cherry pepper – *Heat 1–3 Round chilli about 4 cm/1½ in. in diameter. Bright red with plump flesh and masses of seeds. Sweet in flavour and fairly mild in heat. Grown in Hungary, Europe and California. Ideal for salads.*

Hungarian sweet chilli – *Heat 0–1 About 15 cm/6 in. in length, being broad at the stem with a rounded end. Bright red, mild in heat with a thick flesh, very similar to the bell pepper when used as pimientos. Grown in Hungary, Europe and California. Ideal for any dish where heat is not a requirement.*

Jalapeño – *Heat 5–6 The most commonly used chilli, about 5–7.5 cm/2–3 in. in length, tapering to a rounded end. Either green or, when ripe, yellow or red, all having plump thick flesh and being very fat and juicy. When dried and smoked, known as chipotles. Varying in flavour according to the colour; the green have a distinctive vegetable flavour whereas the ripe chillies are slightly sweeter. Grown in Mexico, Texas and the south-west of America. Ideal for everything: salsas, soups, casseroles, sauces, dips, stuffing or pickles.*

Jamaican hot – *Heat 9 About 5 cm/2 in. in length, bright red and of similar shape to the Scotch bonnet or habanero to which they are related. Thin flesh with a sweet hot flavour. Grown in Jamaica and other Caribbean islands. Ideal for curries, fish stews and chutneys.*

Kalyanpur, Kesanakurru and Kovilpatti – *Heat varies All Indian chillies that are used extensively throughout the country. Green and red.*

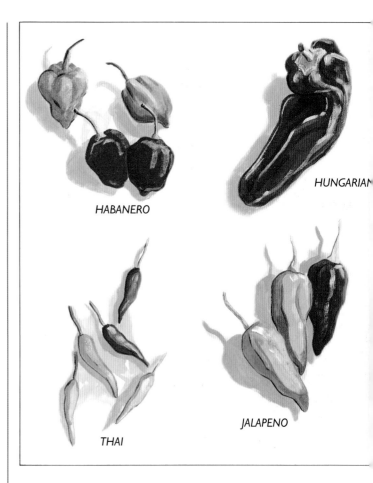

HABANERO

HUNGARIAN

THAI

JALAPENO

Kashmir – *Heat 6–8 Close relation to the jalapeño and serrano chillies, being green or red, about 2.5–5 cm/1–2 in. in length. Also called sriracha or siracha, a sauce is made from these chillies in Thailand and sold around the world as an accompaniment to fish.*

Kenyan – *Heat 2–3 About 2.5–5 cm/1–2 in. in length and similar in appearance to the jalapeño chilli. Bright green, turning red when ripe. Grown in Kenya and surrounding countries.*

Korean – *Heat 6–7 About 7.5–10 cm/3–4 in. in length, thin and slightly curved, tapering to a point. Bright green, thin-fleshed with a hot vegetable flavour. Related to the Thai or bird's eye chilli. Grown in Korea, Japan and California. Ideal for stir-fries, marinades and pickling.*

Macho – *Heat 9–10 Tiny chillies about 6 mm/¼ in. in length. Both green or red. Have a sharp intense flavour and heat and are very hot. Related to the pequín. Grown in South America and Mexico. Ideal for salsas and casseroles.*

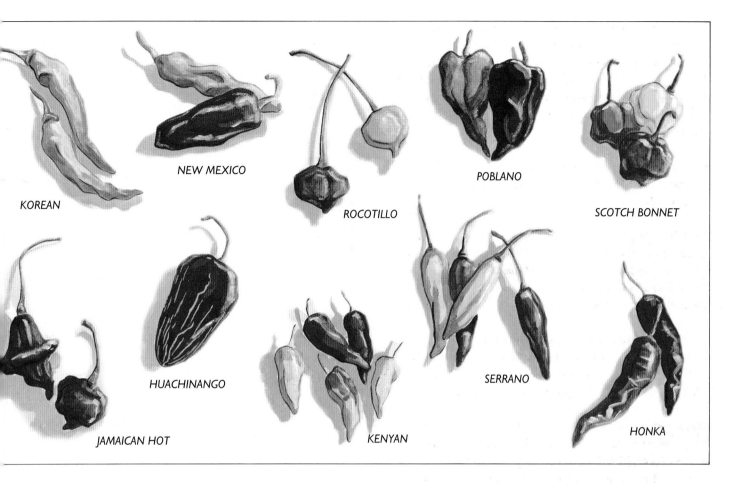

KOREAN

NEW MEXICO

ROCOTILLO

POBLANO

SCOTCH BONNET

JAMAICAN HOT

HUACHINANGO

KENYAN

SERRANO

HONKA

Manzana – Heat 6–8 Also known as chilli rocoto, about 7.5 cm/3 in. in length and is like a mis-shapen bell pepper. Usually yellow or orange with a thick flesh and black seeds. Has a fruity hot flavour. Grown in Central America and Mexico. Ideal for sauces, stuffed or served as a vegetable.

Mundu – Heat 2 A deep red short and stout chilli originating in India. It is very mild in heat.

New Mexico – Heat 3–4 Both green and red, about 15–23 cm/6–9 in. in length. An elongated chilli that varies considerably in heat, having a clear defined chilli flavour. The red variety is fleshy, as is the green, but is far sweeter and known in Mexico as chilli pasado when roasted and dried. These chillies freeze exceptionally well. Grown in New Mexico. Ideal for salsas, sauces, stuffed and casseroles; the red chillies are also used in red chilli and barbecue sauces.

Nigerian – Heat 8–9 About 1–3 cm/⅜–1¼ in. in length with a wrinkled red skin. Grown in Africa.

Peruvian – Heat 7–8 About 5 cm/2 in. in length, like a very small bell pepper in shape. Green, yellow or red. Has a thin flesh with a tropical fruity flavour. Fairly intense in heat. Grown in South America. Ideal for cebiche and salsas.

Peter pepper – Heat 7 About 10 cm/4 in. in length, quite a rare chilli and often grown for its ornamental qualities, being very crinkled in appearance and bright red. Has a sweet hot flavour. Grown in Louisiana and Texas. Ideal for salsas, garnish and as an ornamental house plant.

Poblano – Heat 3 Green or red, about 10–12.5 cm/4–5 in. in length. Thick-fleshed with a medium to hot heat. The green poblano is always cooked prior to eating, and roasting gives both green and red a full earthy flavour. When dried, referred to as ancho and sometimes as pasilla which is in fact incorrect. Grown in central Mexico and California. Ideal for sauces, stuffing, stews and tamales.

Prik Chee Fa – Heat 5–8 A very popular Thai chilli, prik being the Thai name for chilli. A red chilli about 10 cm/4 in. in length and fat in shape.

Rocotillo – *Heat 7 About 2.5 cm/1 in. in length and squat in shape. Related to the Scotch bonnet and habanero. Because of its shape it is referred to as squash chilli as it looks similar to a pattypan. Thin-fleshed with a mild fruit flavour but intense heat. Grown in South America. Ideal for pickling, salsas and sauces.*

Santa Fe Grande – *Heat 6 About 6.5 cm/2½ in. in length. Pale yellow. Thick-fleshed with a light fruity flavour similar to a melon. A type of güero chilli. Medium to hot. Grown in north Mexico and south-west America. Ideal for salsas, pickles and sauces.*

Santaka – *Heat 9 A very straight, thin, deep red chilli. Grown in Japan.*

Scotch Bonnet – *Heat 9–10 About 2.5 cm/1 in. in length, like a squashed Chinese lantern in shape. Pale yellow, green, orange or red with an extremely hot fruity yet smoky flavour. Related to the habanero and Jamaican hot. Grown in Jamaica and other islands of the Caribbean. Ideal for jerk sauces, condiment sauces and Caribbean curries.*

Serrano – *Heat 7 About 5 cm/2 in. in length, smooth with a tapered round end. A thin red or green chilli with a clean biting taste. It has a relatively high heat content, but the ripe red serrano is slightly sweeter than its green counterpart. Can be substituted for the Thai or bird's eye chilli in the ratio of 3 serrano chillies to 1 Thai chilli. Grown in Mexico and the south-west of America. Ideal for guacamole, stir-fries and salsas.*

Tabasco – *Heat 9 About 2.5 cm/1 in. in length, thin-fleshed with a strong biting heat. Bright orange or red and used mainly for making the famous Tabasco sauce. Grown in Louisiana and Central and South America. Used for Tabasco sauce.*

Tepín – *Heat 8 About 6 mm/¼ in. in length, bright orange to red similar in appearance to little chillies and closely related to the wild cherries found in Mexico. Has a fiery heat that is not long-lasting. Grown in South America and desert areas. Ideal for soups and casseroles.*

Thai or Bird's Eye – *Heat 7–8 About 4 cm/1½ in. in length, thin elongated with a pointed end. Thin-fleshed with many seeds and has a fierce heat. Green or red. Grown in Thailand, Asia and California. Ideal for stir-fries and all Asian dishes.*

Usimulagu – *Heat 5–8 A chilli similar in shape to the Thai bird's eye but not as red and slightly milder. Grown in India.*

Dried Chillies

Like wine, dried chillies have many different flavours and it takes a connoisseur to detect the subtle differences. They vary from rich smoky and woody flavours to fruity flavours of cherries, plums or damsons, those that have a distinct citrus flavour and even some with a chocolate, liquorice or coffee flavour. It takes time to develop the palate by learning about the different flavours, but it is time well spent. Chillies can transport an ordinary dish to new culinary heights as their depth and richness in flavour is incomparable.

The drying process intensifies the flavour and gives it a real punch. On drying, the natural sugars concentrate and produce the great depth of flavours that are present.

When buying dried chillies, check that they have no discoloration or spots and are clean, not dirty or dusty. If the chilli is split, much of its oil will have been lost, resulting in an inferior taste. Store in an airtight container for 3–4 months, certainly no longer than 6 months.

Some people recommend deseeding the chilli before roasting and rehydrating, while others do not; obviously the choice is up to the individual. First, lightly roast or dry-fry in a non-stick pan for a few minutes, being careful not to burn or scorch the chilli, otherwise it will taste burnt. Then cover with very hot but never boiling water and leave for at least 10 minutes, or until soft, Drain and then use as described in the recipe. Whether or not you discard the seeds and membrane is a personal choice, but remember the heat is in the membrane, not the seeds.

As with fresh chillies, there are many different varieties of dried chillies and if one is not available, another, or even chilli powder, can be substituted. If powder is used, the flavour will, however, not be as good. Any fresh chilli can be dried but the more obscure varieties are difficult to find other than in their country of origin. Below is a list of the types more commonly available in high quality food stores or specialist shops.

Types of Dried Chillies

If a particular type of chilli is specified in a recipe and is unobtainable, either substitute one of the equivalent heat or use more chillies with a lower heat content.

Ancho – *Heat 3–5 The dried poblano chilli and one of the most commonly available. It has ripened to a deep reddish brown with a wrinkled skin. Not to be confused with the mulato which has a blackish tinge to the skin and is not as sharp or fruity as the ancho. About 12.5 cm/5 in. in length, having a sweet fruit flavour with hints of raisin, coffee and liquorice. The ancho, mulato and* pasilla form the holy trinity of chillies and are used to make the traditional mole sauces. Grown in Mexico and California.

Cayenne – Heat 8 About 5–10 cm/2–4 in. in length, bright red with a thin body tapering to a point. Can be used in sauces and soups and is extensively used in powdered form as seasoning. Grown in Louisiana and Mexico.

Chipotle – Heat 6 A large dried smoked jalapeño, dull tan to coffee brown, about 5–10 cm/2–4 in. in length. Often available in cans or jars, they are hot and normally used with their seeds and membranes intact. The chipotle grande is a dried huachinango chilli which is similar in flavour but larger in size. Grown in South America and Texas.

Guajillo – Heat 2–4 One of the most common dried chillies available, about 10–15 cm/4–6 in. in length with a rough maroon skin. It has a slightly bitter or tannin flavour and the skin is often discarded after rehydration due to its toughness. Grown in north and central Mexico.

Mulato – Heat 3 About 12.5 cm/5 in. in length, a deep dark brown chilli which is round at the stem, tapering to a point. It has a smokier flavour than the ancho and the predominant taste is liquorice with a hint of tobacco and cherry. Like the ancho, it is sold in Mexico in three different grades, varying in depth or taste and quality. Grown in central Mexico.

New Mexico – Heat 2–3 Like the fresh ones, they come in different colours, from olive green (from the green New Mexico chilli) to bright scarlet. Being the same length as their fresh counterparts, they have all the same qualities except the flavour is intensified. They can also be referred to as dried California chilli. Often sold as crushed chilli flakes. Grown in New Mexico and Rio Grande.

Pasilla – Heat 4 Also known as the chilli negro and constitutes the third member of the trinity of chillies required for a traditional mole sauce. About 15 cm/6 in. in length, dark raisin brown to black, shiny and wrinkled. Pasillas range in heat from mild to fairly hot with a hint of grape and liquorice. Apart from being used in mole sauces, the pasilla is also good for many other sauces and blends well with seafood dishes. Can be found in some areas as a powder. Grown in Central Mexico.

> Remember when handling chillies, great care must be exercised. If necessary, use rubber gloves. Wash fresh chillies after deseeding under cold running water and in no circumstances rub your eyes, mouth or nose before you wash your hands.

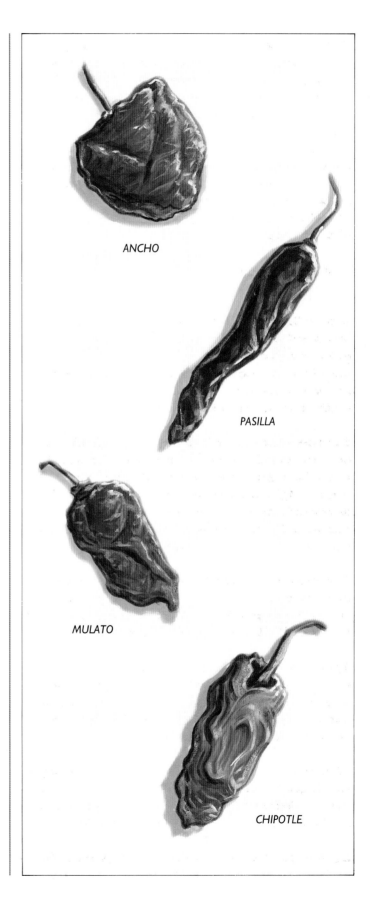

ANCHO

PASILLA

MULATO

CHIPOTLE

Soups

RED PEPPER SOUP

Serves 4

2 Hungarian cherry peppers
(or red bell peppers)
2 tbsp sunflower oil
1 onion, finely chopped
1 garlic clove, crushed
600 ml/1 pt vegetable or
chicken stock
225 g/8 oz ripe tomatoes, peeled
and deseeded
salt and pepper
2 tbsp single cream and chopped
Hungarian cherry pepper, to serve

🌶 Preheat the grill. Wash the peppers and cut in half, discarding the seeds. Place, skin-side uppermost, on a sheet of foil in a grill pan under the grill. Drizzle with 1 tbsp of the oil and grill for 5–10 minutes, or until the skins have blistered. Remove from the heat and allow to cool. When cool, remove the skin and roughly chop.

🌶 Meanwhile, heat the remaining oil in a pan and sauté the onion and garlic for 5 minutes, or until transparent but not browned. Add the chopped peppers and then the stock. Roughly chop the tomatoes and add to the pan with seasoning to taste. Bring to the boil, cover, then simmer gently for 15 minutes, or until the peppers are really soft.

🌶 Allow to cool, then purée in a food processor or sieve. If the soup is to be served hot, return to the rinsed pan, check the seasoning and reheat gently. If it is to be served cold, chill for at least 1 hour.

🌶 To serve, add the cream and swirl lightly, then sprinkle with a little chopped chilli pepper.

BLACK BEAN SOUP

Sopa de frijoles

Serves 4

225 g/8 oz dried black beans
1 tbsp sunflower oil
100 g/4 oz streaky bacon, chopped
1 large onion, chopped
1 garlic clove, crushed
2–3 green jalapeño chillies, deseeded
and chopped
2 tomatoes, peeled and chopped
600 ml/1 pt vegetable or
chicken stock
few sprigs of fresh coriander
salt and pepper
freshly chopped coriander,
to garnish

This soup is sometimes called Poor Man's Soup. Any beans of your choice can be used.

🌶 Cover the black beans with cold water and soak overnight. Next day, drain, put into a large pan, cover with cold water and bring to the boil. Boil rapidly for 15 minutes, then drain and reserve.

🌶 Heat the oil in a large pan and sauté the bacon, onion, garlic and chillies for 5 minutes, stirring occasionally. Add the black beans, tomatoes and stock, and bring to the boil.

🌶 Reduce the heat to a gentle simmer. Add the sprigs of coriander with seasoning to taste and simmer for 1 hour, or until the beans are tender and a thick consistency is reached. Remove the coriander, check the seasoning and serve sprinkled with chopped coriander as a garnish.

TORTILLA SOUP

Sopa de tortilla

Serves 4

1 tbsp corn oil
1 large onion, chopped
2–3 fresno chillies, deseeded
and chopped
2 carrots, cut into julienne strips
750 ml/1¼ pt vegetable or
chicken stock
grated rind and juice of 2 limes
2 courgettes, trimmed and thinly sliced
salt and pepper
taco crisps
freshly chopped coriander and sliced
chilli, to garnish

🌶 Heat the oil in a large pan and sauté the onion and chillies for 5 minutes, or until soft. Add the carrots with the stock and lime rind and juice. Bring to the boil. Reduce the heat, cover and simmer gently for 5 minutes.

🌶 Cut the courgettes into half-moon shapes and add to the pan with seasoning to taste. Cook for a further 3–5 minutes, or until the vegetables are tender. Check the seasoning.

🌶 Place a few taco crisps in the base of four individual soup bowls. Ladle the soup over and serve immediately garnished with chopped coriander and sliced chilli.

Red Pepper Soup ▶

COLD AVOCADO SOUP

Sopa de aguacate

HEAT 2

Serves 4–6

1–2 green Anaheim chillies

1 tbsp oil

3 large ripe avocados

150 ml/¼ pt chicken or vegetable stock

300 ml/½ pt single cream

150 ml/¼ pt milk

1–2 tbsp lime juice

salt and white pepper

freshly snipped chives and soured cream, to garnish

Preheat the grill to high. Cut the chilli in half and discard the seeds. Place in a grill pan, skin-side uppermost, and drizzle with the oil. Grill for 5 minutes, or until the skin has blistered. Remove from the heat and allow to cool.

Discard the skin and membrane from the chilli and roughly chop. Put into a food processor. Peel and stone the avocados, then roughly chop and put into the processor with the stock. Blend to form a smooth purée.

With the machine still running at a low speed, add the cream, then the milk.

Stir in the lime juice and seasoning to taste. Pour into a soup tureen and chill for at least 1 hour. Serve garnished with snipped chives and soured cream.

Serves 4–6

1 tsp oil

1 tsp green curry paste

600 ml/1 pt chicken stock

150 ml/¼ pt coconut milk

1–2 bird's eye (Thai) chillies, deseeded
and chopped

2 lemon grass stalks, outer leaves
removed and finely chopped

4 kaffir lime leaves

2.5 cm/1 in piece root ginger, peeled
and finely grated

350 g/12 oz chicken breasts, skinned
and cut into thin strips

100 g/4 oz green beans, trimmed and
cut into short lengths

7.5 cm/3 in piece cucumber, peeled if
preferred and cut into strips

100 g/4 oz cooked fragrant rice

1–2 tsp clear honey

4 tbsp single cream (optional)

CHICKEN *and* CHILLI SOUP

Heat the oil in a large pan and fry the curry paste gently for 3 minutes stirring occasionally.

Add the stock with the coconut milk, chillies, lemon grass, lime leaves and ginger. Bring to the boil and boil for 3 minutes. Reduce the heat, then add the chicken strips and cook for 5–10 minutes, or until the chicken is cooked.

Add the green beans and cucumber with the rice and honey. Simmer for a further 5 minutes, or until the vegetables are tender.

Stir in the cream, if using, and serve.

HOT *and* SOUR PRAWN SOUP

Serves 4–6

900 ml/1½ pt fish or chicken stock

2 lemon grass stalks

2.5 cm/1 in piece root ginger, peeled and grated

2–3 bird's eye (Thai) chillies, deseeded and chopped

few fresh kaffir lime leaves

1 large carrot, cut into julienne strips

450 g/1 lb raw king-size prawns, shelled and deveined

100 g/4 oz shiitake mushrooms, wiped and sliced

2 tbsp lime juice

1 tbsp Thai fish sauce

1 tsp chilli paste

100 g/4 oz bean sprouts

2 tbsp freshly chopped coriander

This is a very fragrant soup from Thailand. Some recipes use tamarind to give the sour taste, others lime juice.

🌶 Put the stock into a large pan. Remove the outer leaves from the lemon grass and finely chop. Add to the stock with the ginger, chillies and lime leaves. Bring to the boil, then simmer for 10 minutes.

🌶 Add the carrot, prawns and mushrooms to the pan. Simmer for a further 5–8 minutes, or until the prawns have turned pink.

🌶 Mix the lime juice, fish sauce and chilli paste together, then stir into the pan and continue simmering for 1–2 minutes. Add the bean sprouts and chopped coriander, stir once and then serve.

FISH SOUP *with* CHILLIES

Sinigang na isda

Serves 4

1 tbsp oil

1 large onion, finely chopped

1 garlic clove, crushed

2 celery sticks, trimmed and chopped

2 de agua chillies, deseeded and chopped

225 g/8 oz tomatoes, peeled, deseeded and chopped

1 tbsp tomato purée

450 ml/¾ pt fish stock

450 g/1 lb white fish fillets, skinned and cut into bite-sized pieces

salt and pepper

flat-leaf parsley, to garnish

🌶 Heat the oil in a large pan and sauté the onion, garlic, celery and chillies for 5 minutes, or until softened. Add the chopped tomatoes and tomato purée, and sauté for a further 3 minutes.

🌶 Pour in the stock and bring to the boil. Reduce the heat and simmer gently for 10 minutes.

🌶 Add the fish and simmer for a further 5 minutes, or until the fish is cooked. Season to taste and serve garnished with flat-leaf parsley.

Hot and Sour Prawn Soup ▶

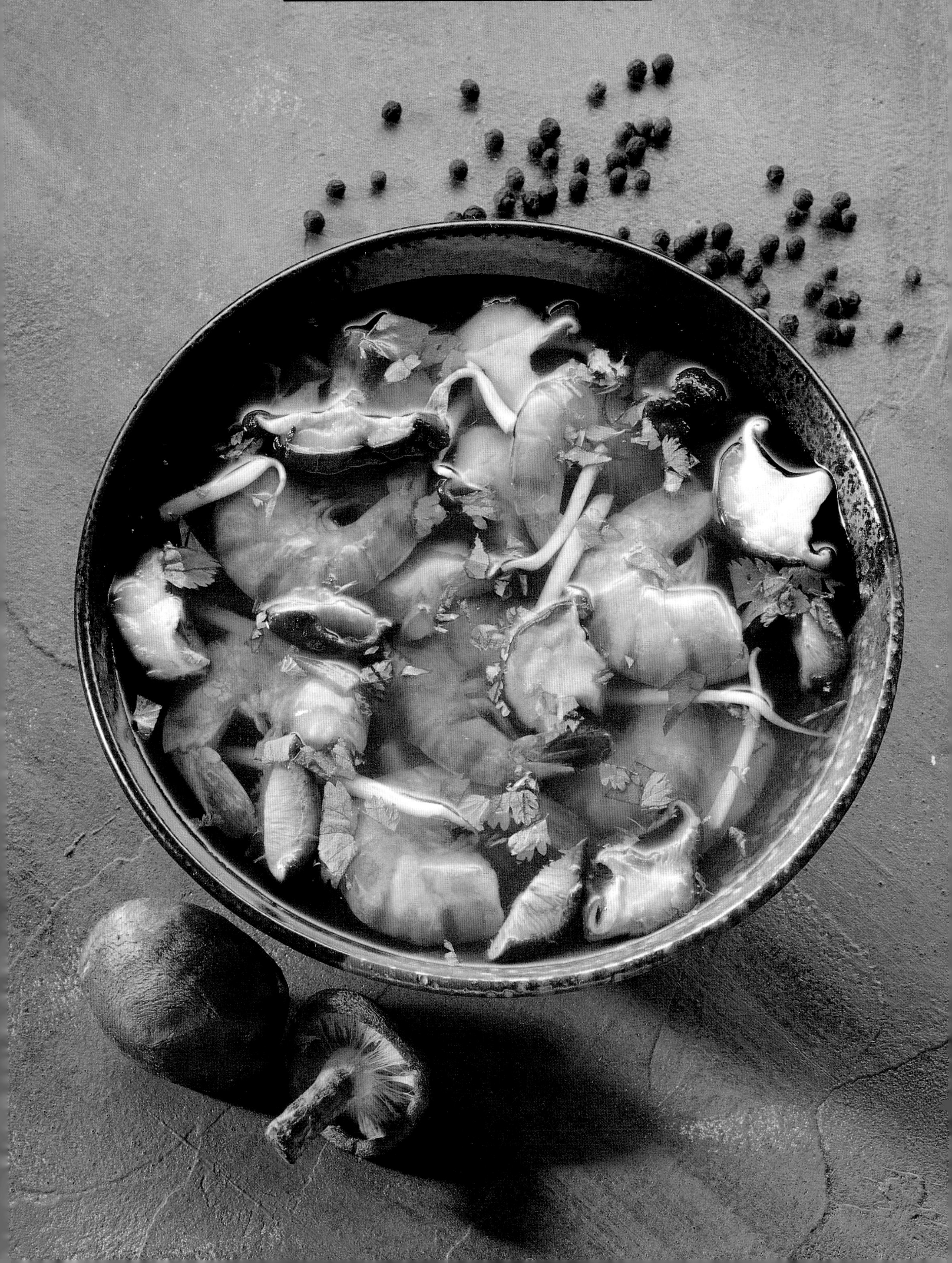

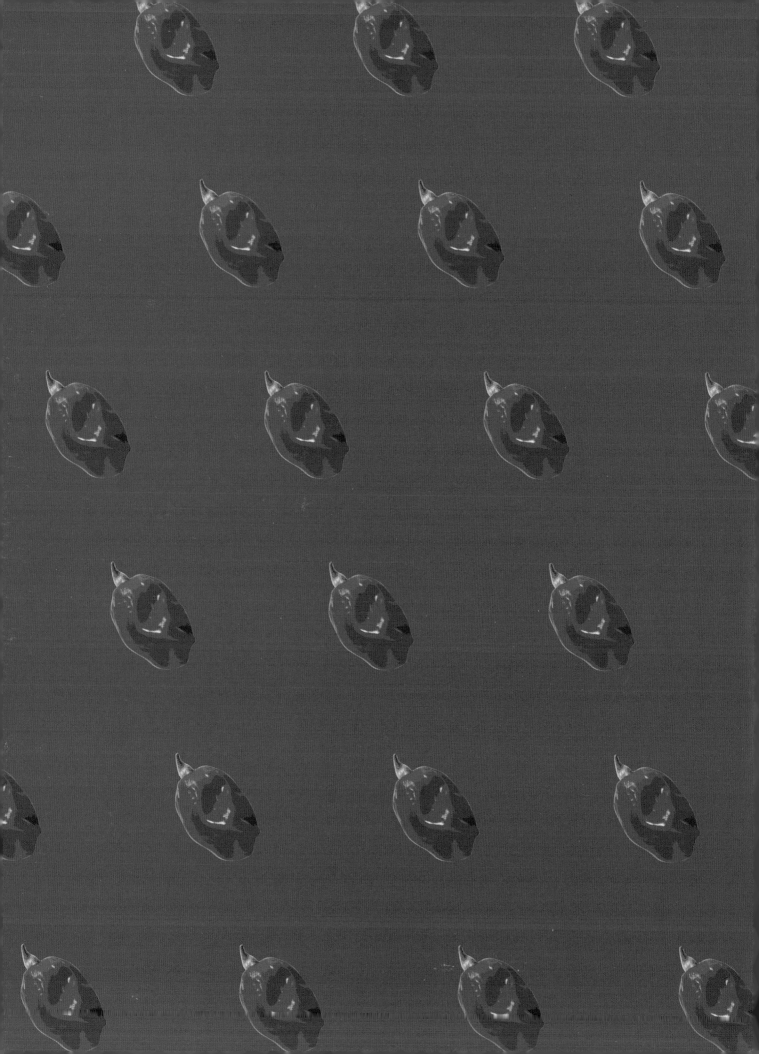

Chapter 2

Starters and Salads

BEAN DIP *with* CHILLI

Serves 6–8

3–4 jalapeño chillies

2 tsp corn or olive oil

200 g/7 oz canned red kidney beans,
   drained and rinsed

200 g/7 oz canned cannellini beans,
   drained and rinsed

1–2 garlic cloves, crushed

4–5 tbsp tomato juice

1 ripe mango, peeled and sliced

1 tbsp freshly chopped oregano

extra freshly chopped oregano,
   to garnish

crudités, to serve

Preheat the grill to high. Place the chillies in a grill pan and drizzle with the oil. Cook for 4–5 minutes, or until the skins have blistered and blackened.

Put the chillies into a polythene bag and leave to sweat for 10 minutes; then discard the skin and seeds if a milder dip is required. Put into a food processor with the remaining ingredients and blend to form a thick dipping consistency.

Turn into a serving dish, cover and chill for 30 minutes to allow the flavours to develop. Serve, sprinkled with chopped oregano, and the crudités.

REFRIED BEANS

Frijoles refritos

Serves 6

225 g/8 oz dried pinto or
   borlotti beans

900 ml/1½ pt beef or chicken stock

1 large onion, chopped

2 garlic cloves, crushed

4 green New Mexico chillies,
   deseeded and chopped

1 tsp salt

black pepper

50 g/2 oz lard or 3–4 tbsp corn
   or olive oil

2 tbsp soured cream (optional)

2 tbsp freshly chopped coriander
   or parsley

Refried beans can also be made with red kidney beans. This is a traditional Mexican dish, but they can also be found in Spain, where "refritos" means thoroughly.

Cover the beans with cold water and leave to soak overnight. Next day rinse and put into a saucepan. Cover with cold water and bring to the boil. Boil rapidly for 15 minutes. Drain again and return the beans to the rinsed pan.

Add the stock, onion, garlic and chillies, and bring to the boil. Reduce the heat and simmer for 1 hour, or until the beans are tender. Drain, reserving the cooking liquor.

Add the salt and pepper to the beans and mash with 4–5 tbsp of the cooking liquor. Alternatively, put into a food processor with the reserved cooking liquor and blend to form a chunky purée.

Heat the lard or oil in a frying pan and add the mashed beans. Cook for about 10-15 minutes or until dry, stirring frequently to prevent the beans from sticking. Stir in the soured cream, if using, and chopped herbs.

GUACAMOLE

Serves 4

2 ripe avocados

225 g/8 oz ripe tomatoes, peeled,
   deseeded and finely chopped

1 bunch spring onions, trimmed and
   finely chopped

2 serrano chillies, deseeded and
   finely chopped

1–2 jalapeño chillies, deseeded and
   finely chopped

2 tbsp lime juice

1½ tbsp freshly chopped coriander

salt and pepper

zested lime rind, to garnish

taco crisps and crudités, to serve

A very traditional Mexican dish, with many different versions. Mexicans will serve Guacamole as a starter, side accompaniment, salad or appetizer with drinks.

🌢 Peel the avocados and discard the stones. Mash the flesh with a potato masher or fork.

🌢 Add the finely chopped tomato and spring onions with the chillies and mix well. Stir in the lime juice with the coriander and seasoning to taste. Turn into a serving bowl and fork the top.

🌢 Sprinkle with the lime zest just before serving with taco crisps and crudités. It is best eaten immediately but if it has to be kept, place one of the avocado stones in the centre, cover and chill for no longer than 1 hour.

HEAT 7–8

Serves 4

Dipping Sauce

2 tbsp Thai fish sauce

2 garlic cloves, crushed

1–2 tbsp sugar

2 tbsp lime juice

2 tbsp white wine vinegar

1 bird's eye (Thai) chilli, deseeded and finely chopped

Parcels

1 tbsp corn or sunflower oil

1 garlic clove, crushed

2 lemon grass stalks, outer leaves removed and finely chopped

2.5 cm/1 in piece root ginger, peeled and grated

2–3 bird's eye (Thai) red chillies, deseeded and chopped

225 g/8 oz chicken breast, skinned and shredded

1 tbsp soy sauce

2 tsp Thai fish sauce

100 g/4 oz bean sprouts

1 small iceburg lettuce, rinsed

HEAT 6–7

Makes 3 x 900 g/2 lb jars

225 g/8 oz aubergines

225 g/8 oz carrots, sliced

225 g/8 oz baby onions

225 g/8 oz beans, trimmed and sliced in half if large

1 red pepper, deseeded and sliced

1 green pepper, deseeded and sliced

2 tbsp salt

3–4 Korean chillies, sliced

1 tsp cumin seeds

1 tsp coriander seeds

1 tsp mixed peppercorns

1 cinnamon stick, bruised

900 ml/1½ pt vinegar

2 garlic cloves, crushed

2 tbsp dark brown sugar

THAI LETTUCE PARCELS

❧ Mix all the ingredients for the sauce together and leave for at least 30 minutes for the flavours to develop.

❧ Heat the oil in a wok or large saucepan and stir-fry the garlic, lemon grass, ginger and chillies for 2 minutes.

❧ Add the chicken and continue to stir-fry for 5 minutes, or until the chicken is cooked.

❧ Add the soy and fish sauce, stir once, then add the bean sprouts and stir-fry for a further 30 seconds.

❧ Arrange spoonfuls of the chicken mixture on a lettuce leaf and drizzle with a little of the sauce. Roll up to form a parcel and serve.

PICKLED SPICY VEGETABLES

❧ Trim the aubergines and cut into small dice. Put into a bowl with the remaining vegetables, sprinkling each layer with salt. Cover and leave overnight.

❧ Put the chillies, spices, vinegar, garlic and sugar into a pan and bring to the boil. Remove from the heat and pour into a clean bowl or jug. Cover and leave for at least 2 hours.

❧ Rinse the vegetables well and drain thoroughly. Then pack into clean sterilized jars. Cover with the vinegar and seal. Keep for 2 weeks before using.

Thai Lettuce Parcels ▶

DEEP-FRIED BRIE *with* SPICY APRICOT SALSA

HEAT 2–3

Serves 4

225 g/8 oz French Brie
1 (size 3) egg, beaten
100 g/4 oz fresh white breadcrumbs
oil for deep-frying

Salsa
1 tbsp sunflower oil
1 small onion, finely chopped
1 Hungarian cherry pepper, deseeded
* and finely chopped*
1 red fresno chilli, deseeded and
* finely chopped*
100 g/4 oz no-need-to-soak apricots,
* finely chopped*
150 ml/¼ pt orange juice
fresh salad leaves, to garnish

➘ Cut the Brie into four equal portions. Dip in the beaten egg, then coat in the breadcrumbs. Cover lightly and place in the refrigerator while preparing the sauce.

➘ Heat the sunflower oil in a pan and gently sauté the onion, cherry pepper and chilli for 5 minutes. Add the apricots and orange juice, and simmer for 15 minutes, or until a chunky consistency is reached.

➘ Heat the oil for deep-frying to 170°C/340°F and fry the Brie for 3–4 minutes, or until golden. Drain on paper towels. Serve with the apricot salsa, garnished with fresh salad leaves.

SHRIMP *and* CHILLI SALAD

HEAT 7–8

Serves 4

1 ripe melon, such as galia or
* ogen, deseeded*
rocket and radicchio leaves
225 g/8 oz peeled shrimps or prawns,
* thawed if frozen*
2 red fresno chillies, deseeded
* and sliced*
few amatista (or fiesta)
* chillies, to garnish*

Dressing
1 tbsp soy sauce
2 tsp clear honey, warmed
salt and pepper
1 tbsp tomato purée
1 red fresno chilli, roasted, deseeded
* and finely chopped*
2 tsp sesame oil
3 tbsp water

➘ Discard the skin of the melon and cut the flesh into thin wedges. Arrange the salad leaves on four individual plates and top with the melon slices and shrimps or prawns. Sprinkle with the sliced chillies.

➘ Put all the ingredients for the dressing into a screw-topped jar. Secure the lid and shake vigorously until well blended. Just before serving, drizzle the dressing over the melon and scatter the whole chillies on top.

◄ *Deep fried Brie with Spicy*
* Apricot Salsa*

WARM *and* SPICY SALAD

HEAT 3–4

Serves 4

4 tbsp oil

2 garlic cloves, crushed

2 chawa chillies, deseeded and sliced

1 tsp ground coriander

1 tsp ground cumin

½ tsp turmeric

1 red onion, cut into thin wedges

1 small red pepper, deseeded and cut into thin strips

175 g/6 oz okra, trimmed and lightly pricked with a fork

225 g/8 oz tomatoes, peeled, deseeded and chopped

100 g/4 oz oyster mushrooms, wiped and sliced

1 tbsp freshly chopped coriander

soured cream, to serve

🌶 Heat the oil in a wok or large pan and stir-fry the garlic and chillies gently for 2 minutes. Add the spices and stir-fry for a further 1 minute.

🌶 Increase the heat slightly, then add the onion and pepper and cook for 2 minutes, stirring frequently. Add the okra, chopped tomatoes and mushrooms and stir-fry for a further 3 minutes, or until the vegetables are cooked but still retain a bite.

🌶 Stir in the chopped coriander and serve on individual plates, topped with spoonfuls of soured cream.

CUCUMBER SALAD *with* CHILLIES

HEAT 5–6

Serves 4

1 large cucumber, peeled

1 small red onion, thinly sliced

2–3 red serrano chillies, deseeded and thinly sliced

2 tbsp lime juice

1 tbsp Thai fish sauce

2 tsp clear honey, warmed

1 tbsp sesame oil

rocket leaves

50 g/2 oz large roasted peanuts, roughly chopped

The dressing for this salad is traditionally made with dried prawns. If using, grind 2 tablespoons of prawns to a fine powder in a pestle and mortar, then add to the dressing and pour over the cucumbers.

🌶 Cut the cucumber in half lengthways and cut into half-moon shapes. Place in a large shallow dish. Scatter over the onion and chilli slices.

🌶 Mix together the lime juice, fish sauce, honey and oil. Pour over the cucumber and leave in a cool place for at least 30 minutes to allow the flavours to develop.

🌶 Arrange the rocket leaves on a serving platter, top with the cucumber mixture and sprinkle with the peanuts.

Cucumber Salad with Chillies ▶

Serves 4

Dressing

6 dried chipotle chillies

1 small onion, sliced

2 garlic cloves, crushed

3 tbsp medium-dry white wine

3 tbsp white wine vinegar

2 tbsp tomato purée

150ml/¼ pt water

Salad

100 g/4 oz rocket

a few small frisée and radicchio leaves

1 small Little Gem lettuce

2 heads red chicory

100 g/4 oz baby spinach leaves

1 small red onion, thinly sliced

3 tbsp assorted fresh herbs, such as
   coriander, flat-leaf parsley,
   oregano and marjoram

MIXED SALAD LEAVES *with* CHIPOTLE CHILLI DRESSING

Chipotle chillies give a delicious smoky flavour to the dressing. You can substitute any other dried chilli if preferred, or use fresno chillies for a fresher flavour.

🌶 Refresh the dried chillies as described on page 16. Split the chillies and discard the seeds. Put into a pan with the remaining dressing ingredients over a gentle heat and cook, covered, for 45 minutes, or until the chillies are soft and liquid is reduced by half.

🌶 Blend to a smooth purée in a blender or food processor and then pass through a sieve to remove any seeds. Reserve.

🌶 Lightly rinse all the salad leaves, the chicory and herbs and pat dry with paper towels. Tear the leaves if large, then toss together in a salad bowl.

🌶 Divide the chicory into single leaves and add to the salad with the onion and herbs. Mix together lightly. Just before serving, drizzle with the dressing and toss lightly.

ONION *and* CHILLI BAHJIS

HEAT 6–7

Serves 4

225 g/8 oz chick-pea or plain flour

1 tsp turmeric

2 tsp ground cumin

2 tsp ground coriander

1 tsp salt

4 green jalapeño chillies, deseeded
and finely chopped

2 garlic cloves, crushed

2 onions, coarsely grated

6 spring onions, trimmed and
finely chopped

about 150 ml/¼ pt iced water

oil for deep-frying

sprigs of fresh coriander, to garnish

❧ Sift the flour, spices and salt into a bowl, then stir in the chopped chillies, garlic, onions and spring onions.

❧ Mix to a soft dropping consistency with the iced water.

❧ Heat the oil to 160°C/320°F and carefully drop in small spoonfuls of the mixture. Cook for 2 minutes, or until golden. Drain on absorbent paper towels and serve garnished with sprigs of coriander.

PICKLED CHINESE LEAVES

HEAT 6

Makes 4 x 450 g/1 lb jars

2 heads Chinese leaves

1 tbsp salt

600 ml/1 pt white wine or rice vinegar

2 tbsp finely chopped, peeled ginger

3 garlic cloves, crushed

300 g/10 oz light soft brown sugar

3–4 Korean chillies, deseeded and
sliced

This is similar to the Korean Kimchi pickle which is designed to "pep up" the appetite. It is traditionally served every day in Korea and northern China.

❧ Rinse the Chinese leaves and cut off the stems. (Use the remaining leaves in salads and stir-fries.) Cut the stems into strips about 5 cm/2 in in length. Place in a colander, sprinkling each layer with salt. Leave to stand for 30 minutes. Rinse thoroughly and drain well. Pack into clean sterilized jars.

❧ Put the vinegar, ginger, garlic, sugar and chillies into a pan and heat until the sugar has dissolved. Bring to the boil and pour over the Chinese leaves. Allow to cool, then cover.

❧ Let the pickle stand at room temperature for 2–4 days before using, pushing the leaves down under the liquid once a day. Allow the air bubbles to escape. Keeps in the refrigerator for up to 1 month. Drain before serving.

Serves 4

4 tbsp corn oil

4 wheat flour or corn tortillas

3 shallots, finely chopped

1 garlic clove, crushed

*1–2 red New Mexico chillies,
    deseeded and chopped*

*225 g/8 oz ripe tomatoes, peeled,
    deseeded and chopped*

1 tbsp tomato purée

2 tbsp water

salt and pepper

4 eggs

4 tbsp refried beans

sprigs of parsley, to garnish

EGGS RANCH STYLE

Huevos rancheros

Heat 1 tsp of the oil in a frying pan and fry a tortilla for 30 seconds on both sides until crisp. Drain and keep warm. Repeat until all the tortillas have been fried.

Heat 2 tbsp of the remaining oil and sauté the shallots, garlic and chillies for 5 minutes. Add the tomatoes and tomato purée blended with the water and leave to simmer while cooking the eggs.

Heat the remaining oil and fry the eggs until cooked as preferred. Place a tortilla on a plate, top with an egg and some tomato sauce. Serve with refried beans and garnish with parsley.

Serves 4

6 tbsp virgin olive oil

1 garlic clove, crushed

2 de agua chillies, deseeded and sliced

2 shallots, thinly sliced

175 g/6 oz assorted wild mushrooms,
  wiped and sliced

100 g/4 oz button mushrooms, wiped

225 g/8 oz plum tomatoes, peeled,
  deseeded and chopped

1 tbsp freshly chopped basil

salt and pepper

1 ciabatta loaf, sliced

Salsa Rojo (page 46)

sprigs of fresh basil, to garnish

Serves 4

100 g/4 oz potatoes, finely diced

1 tbsp corn or sunflower oil

1 onion, finely chopped

1 garlic clove, crushed

2 red Anaheim chillies, deseeded and
finely chopped

1 bird's eye (Thai) chilli, deseeded and
  very finely chopped

1 tsp ground cumin

1 tsp ground coriander

100 g/4 oz peas, thawed if frozen

1 red pepper, deseeded and diced

1 tbsp apricot or fruit chutney

1 tbsp freshly chopped coriander

4 sheets filo pastry

oil for deep-frying

chilli flowers (page 11) and fresh
  coriander, to garnish

SAUTÉED MUSHROOMS *with* CHILLI SALSA

Heat 4 tbsp of the oil in a frying pan and gently sauté the garlic, chillies and shallots for 5 minutes, or until the shallots are soft and transparent.

Add the mushrooms and continue to cook for 4–5 minutes. Stir in the tomatoes, basil and seasoning to taste and heat through for 1–2 minutes.

Meanwhile, drizzle the ciabatta slices with the remaining oil and toast lightly. Arrange the mushroom mixture on the toasted bread and serve with Salsa Rojo. Garnish with sprigs of basil.

VEGETABLE SAMOSAS

Cook the diced potatoes in boiling salted water for 5–8 minutes, or until just cooked, Drain and reserve.

Heat the corn or sunflower oil in a frying pan and gently sauté the onion, garlic and chillies for 3 minutes. Add the spices and sauté for a further 3 minutes.

Remove from the heat and stir in the potatoes, peas, red pepper, chutney and chopped coriander. Mix together well.

Cut the filo pastry sheets in half lengthways to make 8 strips, 25 x 10 cm/10 x 4 in. Place 1½ tbsp of the filling at one end of each strip and fold over diagonally to form a triangle. Continue folding along the strip, sealing the edges with water.

Heat the oil to 160°C/320°F and fry the samosas in batches for about 5 minutes, or until golden. Drain on paper towels. Serve hot or cold garnished with chilli flowers and sprigs of coriander.

Sautéed Mushrooms with Chilli Salsa ▶

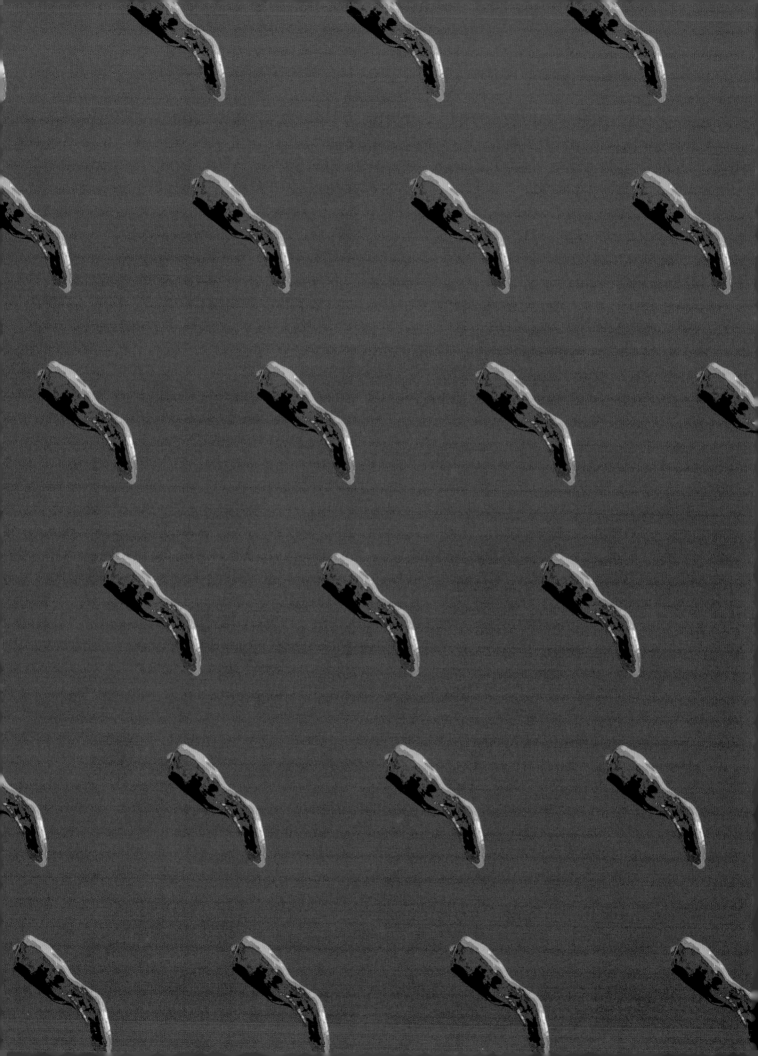

Chapter 3

Sauces and
Relishes

CHILLI MAYONNAISE

HEAT 4–5

Makes 200 ml/7 fl oz

2 (size 3) egg yolks
½–1 tsp salt
½–1 tsp mustard powder
½–1 tsp Red Chilli Paste (page 47)
¼ tsp freshly ground pepper
150 ml/¼ pt olive oil
1–2 tbsp strained lime juice

Put the egg yolks, salt, pepper, mustard powder and Red Chilli Paste into a food processor and switch on to a low speed. Add the olive oil, drop by drop to begin with, then as the mayonnaise thickens, increase to a very thin steady stream. If the mayonnaise is becoming too thick, add a little lime juice.

When all the oil has been added, stir in the lime juice. Cover and chill until required. Use within 1 week of making.

CHILLI SEASONING

HEAT 5

Makes 4-5 tbsps

2 dried ancho chillies
6 dried ají mirasol chillies
1 tsp paprika pepper
3 tbsp coarse sea salt
finely grated rind of 1 lemon

Discard the stems and seeds from the chillies, then place in a non-stick frying pan and fry gently for 3 minutes, shaking the pan occasionally to ensure they do not burn.

Remove from the heat, put the chillies into a bowl and cover with almost boiling water. Cover and leave for 15–20 minutes. Drain and pat dry with paper towels until thoroughly dry.

Place in a pestle and mortar or a coffee grinder and pound to a paste. Add the paprika, salt and lemon rind and continue to grind until a fine consistency is reached.

Pack into small containers, cover and use as required. Store in a cool dark place.

CHILLI BUTTER

HEAT 2–3

Makes 100 g/4 oz

100 g/4 oz unsalted butter, softened
1 green fresno chilli, deseeded and
  finely chopped
1–2 tsp lime juice
1–2 tsp Chilli Seasoning (see above)
1 tbsp freshly chopped coriander

Ideal for use with corn on the cob, fish, steaks, chicken and pork dishes.

Put all the ingredients into a bowl and beat until thoroughly blended.

Shape into a 2.5 cm/1 in roll and wrap in greaseproof paper. Chill until required.

HEAT 8–9

Serves 4

1 tbsp corn or olive oil

1 onion, finely chopped

2 garlic cloves, crushed

2 Scotch bonnet chillies, deseeded
and chopped

2 celery sticks, trimmed and
finely chopped

350 g/12 oz minced beef

1 tbsp tomato purée

2 tbsp water

225 g/8 oz ripe tomatoes, peeled
and chopped

1 tsp ground coriander

1 tsp ground cumin

2 tbsp cider vinegar

1 tsp clear honey

2 tbsp freshly chopped oregano

SPICY MINCED BEEF SAUCE

Picadillo

*Kenyan chillies could be used in this dish if
available, for a milder sauce. Use in tacos,
enchiladas or burritos, over pasta or with rice.*

➥ Heat the oil in a frying pan and sauté the
onion, garlic, chillies and celery for 5 minutes.
Add the beef and cook, stirring frequently, for
5–8 minutes, or until browned.

➥ Blend the tomato purée with the water and
add to the pan with the remaining ingredients.
Bring to the boil, then reduce the heat and
simmer for 45 minutes, or until a thick
consistency is reached.

HEAT 7–8

Makes 350 ml/12 fl oz

3 red serrano chillies

1 tbsp corn or olive oil

4 ripe tomatoes, peeled, deseeded
  and chopped

4 shallots, finely chopped

2 garlic cloves, chopped

1 tsp ground cumin

1 tsp ground coriander

150 ml/¼ pt vegetable or chicken
  stock

2 tbsp tomato purée

½ tsp salt

½ tsp freshly ground pepper

1 tbsp lime juice

2 tbsp freshly chopped coriander

RED CHILLI SAUCE

Salsa rojo

*Both Green and Red Chilli Sauce are used as
a condiment to fish, meat and poultry or can
be used as a dip.*

🌶 Preheat the grill. Place the chillies in the
grill pan and drizzle with the oil. Grill for
5 minutes, or until blackened and blistered.
Put into a polythene bag and leave to
sweat for 10 minutes, then discard the
skins and chop.

🌶 Put all the ingredients, except the
coriander, into a food processor and blend
to a thick consistency.

🌶 Pour into a frying pan and cook over a
gentle heat, stirring frequently for 10 minutes.
(Add a little extra stock or water if consistency
is too thick.)

(Clockwise from top left) ▶
*Red Chilli Paste, Chilli Pepper Relish,
Green Chilli Sauce, Red Chilli Sauce*

GREEN CHILLI SAUCE

Salsa verde

HEAT 4–5

Makes 450 ml/¾ pt

450 g/1 lb green Anaheim chillies
1 large onion, quartered
3 garlic cloves, peeled
2 tbsp corn or olive oil
300 ml/½ pt chicken or
  vegetable stock
1 tsp salt
½ tsp black pepper
2 tbsp freshly chopped coriander
thinly sliced chilli to garnish

Ideal to serve with egg dishes, chicken or as the basis of a stew or casserole.

Preheat the grill. Place the chillies, onion and garlic in the grill pan and drizzle with the oil. Grill for 5–8 minutes, or until the chillies have blistered and the skins blackened. Put the chillies into a polythene bag and leave to sweat for about 10 minutes, then discard the skins.

Put the chillies and all the other ingredients, except the coriander, into a food processor and blend to form a chunky purée. Stir in the coriander and warm through just before serving, garnish with sliced chilli.

CHILLI PEPPER RELISH

HEAT 7–8

Makes 300 ml/½ pt

225 g/8 oz ripe tomatoes, peeled,
  deseeded and chopped
2 shallots, finely chopped
2–3 red serrano chillies, deseeded
  and chopped
1 garlic clove, crushed
1 tsp salt
3 tbsp freshly chopped coriander
1 tbsp lime juice or cider vinegar
7.5 cm/3 in piece cucumber, peeled
  and finely chopped
1 tbsp pumpkin seeds, roasted and
  then finely ground
coriander sprigs to garnish

If liked, this can be served as an appetizer with crudités and taco chips.

Put the tomatoes into a bowl and stir in the shallots, chillies, garlic, salt, coriander and lime juice or vinegar. Mix together well, then cover and leave for at least 30 minutes to allow the flavours to develop.

Stir in the cucumber and pumpkin seeds. Garnish with the coriander sprigs.

RED CHILLI PASTE

HEAT 9

Makes 5 tbsps

4 red habanero chillies, deseeded
1 onion, chopped
2 garlic cloves, crushed
2 tsp ground coriander
1 tbsp freshly chopped coriander
2.5 cm/1 in piece root ginger, peeled
  and grated
grated rind and juice of 2 limes
1 tsp salt
½ tsp black pepper
3 tbsp corn or olive oil

Not suitable for freezing, use when extra heat is required in order to spice up soups, stews and casseroles. Add towards the end of cooking time to give a distinctive and fiery flavour.

Rinse the chillies and put into the top of a steamer over a pan of gently steaming water.

Steam for 5 minutes or until soft. Alternatively, cover with boiling water and leave for 15 minutes, then drain.

Put all the ingredients into a food processor and blend to form a thick paste, adding a little extra oil if necessary. Transfer to a screw-topped jar and store in the refrigerator. Use within 1 week.

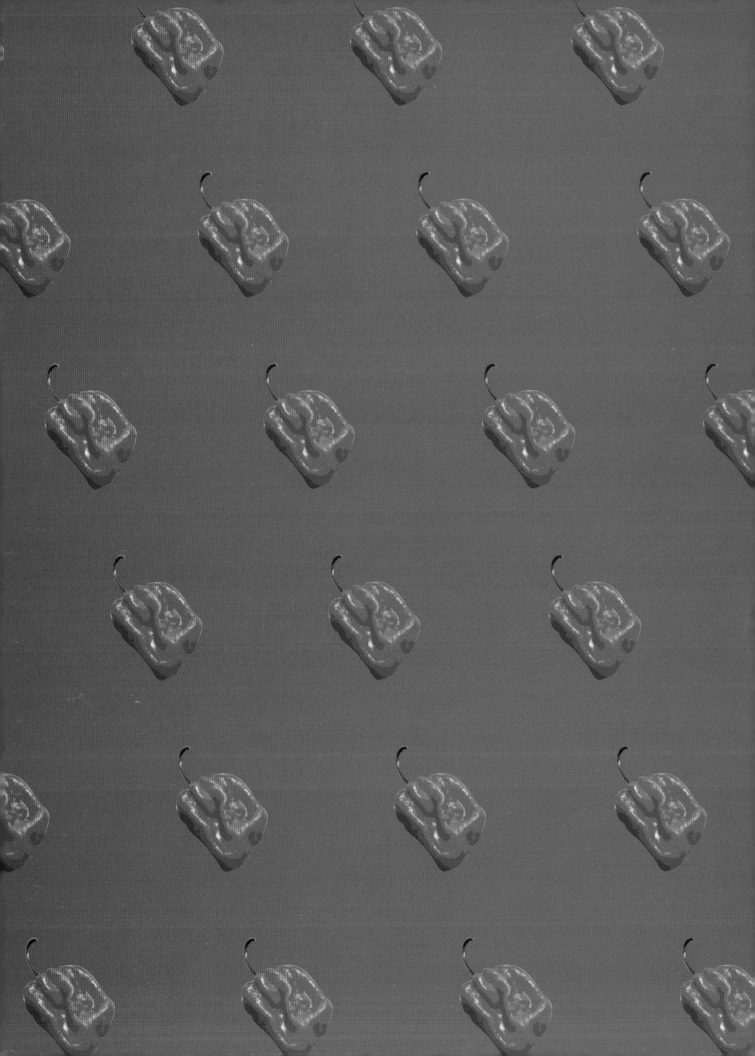

Chapter 4

Potatoes
and Rice

Serves 4

675 g/1½ lb potatoes, cut into chunks

salt and pepper

2 tbsp milk

25 g/1 oz butter

4 red Anaheim chillies, peeled,
  deseeded and finely chopped

6 spring onions, trimmed and
  finely chopped

extra chopped spring onions,
  to garnish

Serves 4

1 large or 2 medium fresh pineapple

2 tbsp sunflower oil

1 red pepper, deseeded and chopped

225 g/8 oz courgettes, trimmed
  and diced

6 spring onions, trimmed and
  sliced diagonally

300 g/10 oz cooked long-grain rice

6 canned jalapeño chillies, drained
  and chopped

salt and pepper

2 tbsp pine kernels, toasted

3 tbsp freshly chopped coriander

grated cheese, to serve

Serves 4

2 tbsp sunflower oil

3 red New Mexico chillies, roasted,
  deseeded and chopped

225 g/8 oz cooked long-grain rice

100 g/4 oz peas, blanched

salt

100 g/4 oz peeled prawns,
  thawed if frozen

2 (size 3) eggs, beaten

2 spring onions, trimmed and chopped

SAVOURY MASHED POTATOES

Cook the potatoes in boiling salted water for 15 minutes, or until tender. Drain, then add the seasoning and milk, and mash until smooth.

Melt the butter in a large pan and gently sauté the chillies and spring onions for 3 minutes.

Add the mashed potatoes and stir well. Heat through for 5–6 minutes, stirring occasionally, until piping hot. Place in a serving dish and fork the top. Sprinkle with a little extra chopped spring onions. Serve immediately.

PINEAPPLE *and* CHILLI RICE

Cut the pineapple in half lengthways through the plume and scoop out the flesh. Reserve the two halves. Discard the central core, dice the remaining flesh and reserve.

Heat the oil in a pan and sauté the red pepper and courgettes for 5 minutes, or until softened. Add the spring onions and sauté for a further 1 minute. Stir in the rice with the canned chillies, seasoning and the reserved pineapple flesh.

Heat gently, stirring occasionally, for 5 minutes, or until hot. Then stir in the pine kernels and coriander. Pile into the reserved pineapple shells and serve with grated cheese.

FRIED CHILLI RICE

The staple food ingredient of the Chinese is rice which forms the basis of much of their traditional cuisine. If preferred, use Thai or Korean chillies, but as they are fiercer in heat, either reduce the quantity or be prepared for a taste explosion.

Heat the oil in a large frying pan and gently sauté the chillies for 1 minute. Add the cooked rice and heat through, stirring frequently, for 3 minutes.

Stir in the peas, salt and prawns, then pour over the eggs and increase the heat. Cook, stirring constantly, for 2–3 minutes, or until the eggs have set. Serve immediately, sprinkled with the chopped spring onions.

Pineapple and Chilli Rice ▶

RED RICE

Arroz rojo

Serves 4

2 tbsp sunflower oil

1 red onion, chopped

2 garlic cloves, chopped

5 red Anaheim chillies, deseeded
   and chopped

6 sun-dried tomatoes, chopped

750–900 ml/1¼–1½ pt
   vegetable stock

175 g/6 oz long-grain rice

1 red pepper, deseeded and chopped

2 tbsp tomato purée

salt and pepper

100 g/4 oz sweetcorn kernels

freshly chopped coriander, to garnish

🌶 Preheat the oven to 180°C/350°F/Gas Mark 4.

🌶 Heat the oil in a pan and gently sauté the onion, garlic, chillies and sun-dried tomatoes for 3 minutes. Add 300 ml/½ pt of the stock and simmer for 10 minutes, or until the tomatoes are soft. Blend in a food processor, then transfer to a frying pan.

🌶 Add the rice, red pepper and the tomato purée blended with 2 tbsp of the stock. Put into a flameproof casserole with 450 ml/¾ pt of the stock and seasoning to taste.

🌶 Bring to the boil, then cover and place in the oven. Cook for 30 minutes. Add the sweetcorn kernels with extra stock if necessary and cook for a further 10 minutes, or until the rice is cooked. Separate the grains with a fork and serve sprinkled with the coriander.

GREEN RICE

Arroz verde

Serves 4

2 tbsp sunflower oil

1 large onion, chopped

2 garlic cloves, chopped

4 green Anaheim chillies, deseeded
   and sliced

175 g/6 oz long-grain white rice

1 green pepper, deseeded and
   chopped

600 ml/1 pt vegetable stock

salt and pepper

100 g/4 oz frozen peas

1 tbsp freshly chopped parsley

2 tbsp pumpkin seeds, toasted

Rice forms a staple part of many different cuisines, offering a nutritious yet relatively cheap food. In all countries where rice grows abundantly, many different recipes have been evolved, all using other ingredients that are plentiful to the relevant country.

🌶 Heat the oil in a large frying pan and sauté the onion, garlic and chillies for 3 minutes. Add the rice and green pepper, and sauté for a further 3 minutes.

🌶 Pour in the stock and bring to the boil. Reduce the heat and simmer for 15 minutes, or until the rice is almost tender. Add a little more stock if necesary and stir occasionally during cooking.

🌶 Stir in the peas and seasoning to taste, and cook for a further 5–7 minutes, or until the rice and peas are cooked. Adjust the seasoning and serve sprinkled with the parsley and toasted pumpkin seeds.

◀ *Arroz Rojo*
   Arroz Verde

HEAT 5

Serves 6

2 tbsp sunflower oil

2 garlic cloves, crushed

4 red de agua chillies, deseeded
  and chopped

175 g/6 oz short-grain rice

1 large carrot, grated

2 tbsp tomato purée

2 tbsp water

600 ml/1 pt vegetable stock

salt and pepper

200 g/7 oz can red kidney beans,
  drained and rinsed

75 g/3 oz sweetcorn kernels

2 tbsp freshly chopped coriander

2 tsp olive oil

1 large tomato, sliced

6 baps, lightly toasted

Chilli Pepper Relish (page 47), to serve

HEAT 6

Serves 4

1 tsp cumin seeds

1 tsp whole coriander

1 tsp fenugreek seeds

5 cloves

6 cardamom pods

2 tbsp sunflower oil

1 large onion, sliced

2 garlic cloves, crushed

4 red jalapeño chillies, deseeded
  and chopped

675 g/1½ lb potatoes, cubed

600 ml/1 pt vegetable stock

1 red pepper, skinned, deseeded
  and sliced

2 tbsp freshly chopped coriander

CHILLI RICE BURGERS

Heat the sunflower oil in a frying pan and sauté the garlic and chillies for 5 minutes. Add the rice and continue to cook for 3 minutes, stirring occasionally. Stir in the carrot.

Blend the tomato purée with the water and stir into the pan with the stock. Add seasoning and bring to the boil. Reduce the heat and simmer for 20 minutes, or until the rice is cooked, stirring occasionally and adding a little extra stock if the rice is very dry.

Add the kidney beans and sweetcorn, and cook for a further 5 minutes. (The mixture needs to be very stiff so that it will stick together.) Stir in the chopped coriander and remove from the heat. Allow to cool.

When the mixture is cool enough to handle, wet your hands slightly and shape into six large burgers. Cover and chill for at least 30 minutes.

Preheat the grill to medium. Place the burgers under the grill and brush lightly with a little olive oil. Grill for 4–5 minutes, or until heated through, carefully turning the burgers over once during cooking.

Place a slice of tomato on the base of each bap and top with a rice burger. Spoon over a little relish, cover with the bap tops and serve with extra Chilli Pepper Relish.

POTATO CURRY

Put the whole spices in a pestle and mortar or food processor and grind to a powder.

Heat the oil in a large pan and sauté the onion, garlic and chillies for 5 minutes, or until softened. Add the ground spices and cook gently for a further 3 minutes, stirring occasionally.

Add the potatoes with the stock and bring to the boil. Cover the pan, reduce the heat and simmer for 15 minutes, or until the potatoes are tender.

Add the sliced red pepper and cook for a further 5 minutes. Stir in the freshly chopped coriander and serve immediately.

Serves 4

675 g/1½ lb potatoes, cut into
  small cubes
1 large onion, sliced
2 garlic cloves, chopped
5 red fresno chillies
4–5 tbsp olive oil
salt and pepper
100 g/4 oz raw peanuts, shelled
shavings of grated Parmesan cheese

POTATOES *with* CHILLI, PEANUTS AND CHEESE

Preheat the oven to 200°C/400°F/Gas Mark 6.

Put the potatoes in a roasting tin and scatter over the onion and garlic.

Make a slit down each chilli and discard the seeds. Chop roughly. Add to the vegetables and sprinkle with the oil, then add the seasoning. Turn the vegetables in the oil and roast in the oven for 50 minutes, turning the vegetables occasionally.

Scatter the peanuts over and continue to roast until cooked and golden. Serve sprinkled with Parmesan cheese.

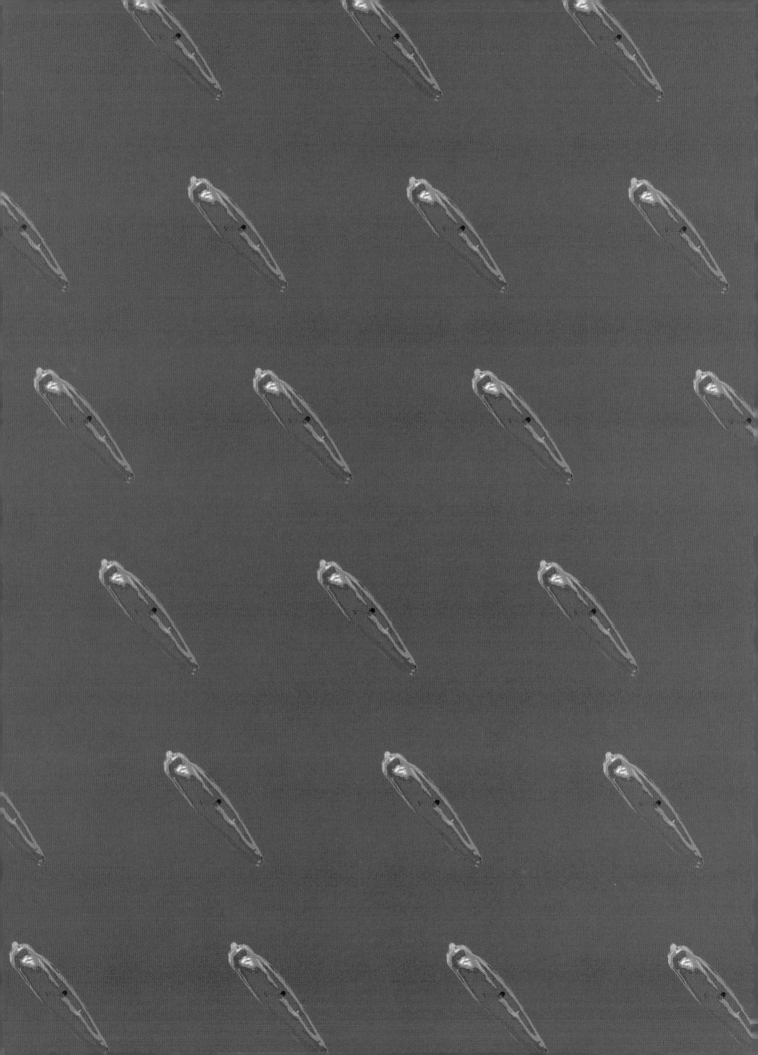

Chapter 5

Fish

SALMON STEAKS *with* THAI STYLE SAUCE

HEAT 5

Serves 4

4 salmon steaks, about
  175 g/6 oz each
1 small onion, sliced
2 bay leaves
few sprigs of parsley
4–5 peppercorns
150 ml/¼ pt dry white wine
1 tbsp white wine vinegar
150 ml/¼ pint water

Sauce
2 tbsp olive oil
1 garlic clove, crushed
2.5 cm/1 in. piece root ginger, peeled
  and grated
100 g/4 oz raw peanuts, shelled
2 red Thai chillies, deseeded and sliced
2 tsp dark brown sugar
300 ml/½ pt vegetable stock
1 tbsp lemon juice
lemon twists to garnish

Wipe the salmon and reserve. Place the onion, bay leaves, parsley, peppercorns, wine and vinegar in a frying pan. Add the water and bring to the boil. Reduce the heat and simmer for 10 minutes. Strain and reserve the liquor until ready to cook the fish.

Heat the oil for the sauce in the frying pan and sauté the garlic and ginger for 2 minutes. Add the peanuts and fry gently for 10 minutes, or until golden.

Put the peanuts and chillies with garlic, ginger and oil in a food processor with the remaining sauce ingredients. Blend to a purée, then return to the cleaned pan and simmer for 8–10 minutes, or until reduced slightly. Keep warm while cooking the fish.

When ready to cook the fish, reheat the reserved liquor in the frying pan and add the fish. Bring to the boil, then cover and reduce the heat to a very gentle simmer. Cook for 3–4 minutes, or until the fish is cooked. Drain and arrange on serving plates and spoon over a little of the sauce. Garnish with lemon twists.

CRAB *in* RICH COCONUT MILK SAUCE

HEAT 4–5

Serves 4

2 garlic cloves, crushed
4 shallots, finely chopped
2.5 cm/1 in piece root ginger,
  peeled and grated
3 red fresno chillies, deseeded and
  finely chopped
6 ajlí mirasol dried chillies, roasted
  and rehydrated (page 16)
2 tbsp corn or sunflower oil
450 g/1 lb white crab meat,
  drained if canned
150 ml/¼ pt coconut milk
1 tbsp cornflour
2 tbsp water
150 ml/¼ pt crème fraîche
chilli flowers (page 11) and lemon
  wedges, to garnish

Put the garlic, shallots, ginger, fresh and rehydrated dried chillies into a food processor and blend to a paste. Alternatively, use a pestle and mortar.

Heat the oil in a wok or large pan and gently fry the paste for 3 minutes, taking care not to burn it. Add the crab meat and heat through for 3 minutes, stirring frequently.

Pour in the coconut milk and bring to the boil. Blend the cornflour to a smooth paste with the water and stir into the crab meat mixture. Cook, stirring constantly, until the sauce thickens. Add the crème fraîche and heat through for 1–2 minutes. Garnish with chilli flowers and lemon wedges, and serve with plenty of warm crusty bread.

Salmon Steaks with ▶
Thai Style Sauce

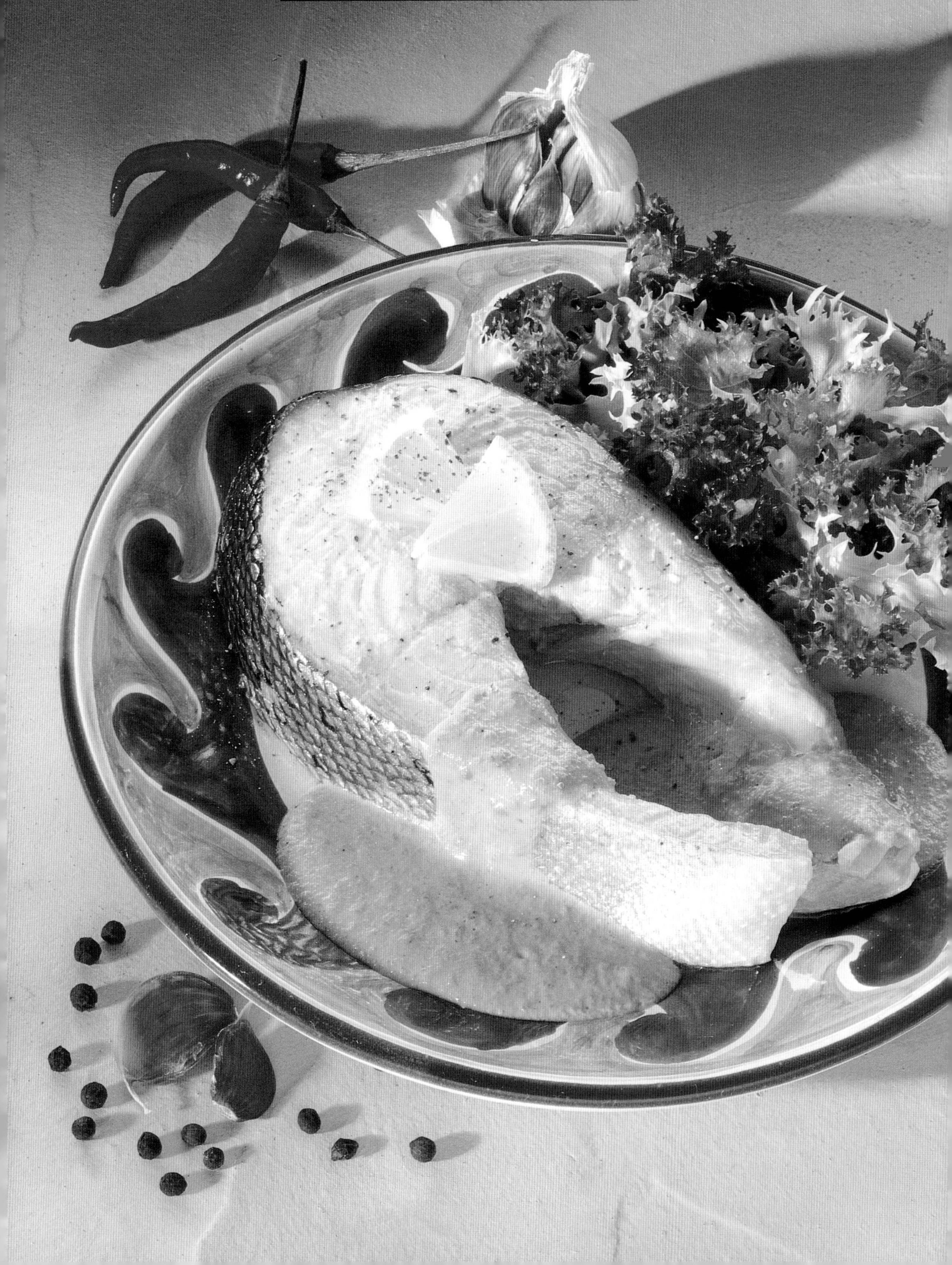

SEAFOOD GUMBO

HEAT 7–8

Serves 4

2 tbsp corn or sunflower oil

1 large onion, chopped

2 garlic cloves, crushed

2–3 Jamaican hot chillies, deseeded
  and chopped

2 celery sticks, trimmed and chopped

2 red peppers, deseeded and sliced

100 g/4 oz back bacon, chopped

2 tbsp filé powder or flour

3 smoked pork sausages or Italian
  sausages, cut into chunks

225 g/8 oz tomatoes, peeled
  and chopped

225 g/8 oz okra, trimmed and sliced

600 ml/1 pt chicken stock

225 g/8 oz monkfish, central bone
  and skin removed and cubed

225 g/8 oz raw prawns, shelled
  and deveined

225 g/8 oz squid, prepared (page 66)
  and sliced

½–1 tsp Tabasco sauce

salt and pepper

175 g/6 oz freshly cooked
  long-grain rice

2 tbsp freshly chopped parsley to
  garnish the rice

Gumbos vary from region to region; there are no hard and fast rules. One of the staple ingredients is okra or lady's fingers. The filé powder is used as a thickening agent; plain flour can be used instead.

Heat the oil in a large pan and gently sauté the onion, garlic, chillies and celery for 5 minutes, or until soft.

Add the sliced red peppers and the bacon, and sauté for a further 3 minutes. Sprinkle in the filé powder or flour and cook gently for a further 3 minutes.

Add the sausages, tomatoes, okra and stock, and bring to the boil. Reduce the heat and simmer for 10 minutes, stirring occasionally. Add the monkfish and simmer for a further 10 minutes, or until the fish is almost tender.

Stir in the prawns, squid, Tabasco sauce and seasoning to taste, and cook for 5–7 minutes, or until all the fish is cooked. (Take care not to overcook the squid.) Finally add the rice and parsley. Heat through for 5–7 minutes and serve.

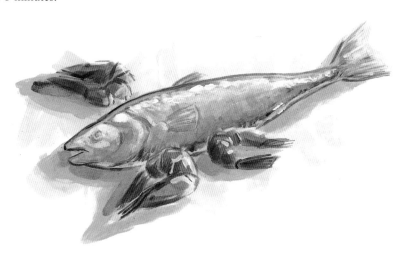

ROAST MONKFISH

HEAT 5–6

Serves 4

675 g/1½ lb piece monkfish, skinned

4 red fresno chillies, deseeded and
  cut into strips

1 red onion, sliced

3 large carrots, sliced

6 celery sticks, trimmed and chopped

2–3 fresh bay leaves

salt and pepper

2 tbsp sunflower or olive oil

150 ml/¼ pt fish or vegetable stock

freshly chopped parsley and
  thinly sliced, deseeded red fresno
  chilli, to garnish

Preheat the oven to 180°C/350°F/Gas Mark 4.

Using a sharp knife, cut the monkfish away from the bone that runs down its centre and discard the bone. Rinse and pat dry with paper towels. Then make small slits down the monkfish fillets on all sides and insert the strips of chilli.

Place the vegetables with the bay leaves on a large sheet of foil and place the fish on top.

Season with salt and pepper. Pour over the oil and stock, and fold the foil over, completely encasing the fish. Place in a roasting tin.

Bake for 20–25 minutes, or until the fish is cooked. Baste occasionally during cooking. Discard the bay leaves and serve garnished with the cooked vegetables.

◀ *Seafood Gumbo*

HEAT 3-4

Serves 6

225 g/8 oz prepared shortcrust pastry

1 tbsp corn or sunflower oil

1 onion, finely chopped

2–3 red Anaheim chillies, deseeded
   and sliced

100 g/4 oz back bacon, cut into strips

225 g/8 oz white crab meat, flaked

100 g/4 oz peeled prawns, thawed
   if frozen

2 (size 3) eggs

150 ml/¼ pt single cream

salt and pepper

HEAT 5-6

Serves 4

8–12 canned large green chillies,
   drained

225 g/8 oz peeled prawns, thawed if
   frozen and finely chopped

4 spring onions, trimmed and chopped

3 green jalapeño chillies, deseeded and
   finely chopped

50 g/2 oz grated hard cheese, such as
   Cheddar

1 small red apple, cored and finely
   chopped

grated rind of 1 lemon

salt and pepper

3–4 tbsp prepared mayonnaise

salad leaves and sliced red jalapeño
   chillies, to garnish

SHELLFISH CHILLI QUICHE

🌶 Preheat the oven to 200°C/400°F/Gas Mark 6.

🌶 Roll the pastry out on a lightly floured surface and use to line a 20 cm/8 in loose-bottomed flan tin. Place a sheet of greaseproof paper and baking beans in the base and bake blind for 12 minutes. Remove the paper and beans and continue baking for a further 5 minutes. Reduce the oven temperature to 180°C/350°F/Gas Mark 4.

🌶 Meanwhile, heat the oil in a frying pan and sauté the onion and chillies for 2 minutes. Add the bacon and sauté for a further 3 minutes. Drain, then arrange the bacon mixture on the base of the flan case.

🌶 Place the crab meat on top of the bacon mixture with the prawns. Beat the eggs with the cream and seasoning to taste, and pour over the crab meat. Bake for 20–25 minutes, or until set.

PRAWN RELLENOS

Rellenos is a Spanish word meaning stuffed. If canned chillies are unavailable, use large fresh ones that have been deseeded and blanched.

🌶 Pat the canned chillies dry with paper towels and make a slit down one side. Discard the seeds if necessary, then rinse and pat dry again.

🌶 Mix the prawns, spring onions, chillies, cheese, apple and lemon rind together with seasoning to taste. Add the mayonnaise and mix together well.

🌶 Using the prawn mixture to stuff the chillies. Arrange on a serving platter and garnish with salad leaves and chillies.

Prawn Rellenos ▶

HEAT 4–5

Serves 4

24 live clams, scrubbed and any open
   ones discarded

1 tbsp sunflower oil

1 red onion, thinly sliced

4 de agua red chillies, deseeded
   and sliced

zested rind of 1 lime

2.5 cm/1 in. piece root ginger, peeled
   and grated

2 garlic cloves, crushed

1 tbsp Thai fish sauce

4 tbsp coconut milk

300 ml/½ pt fish or vegetable stock

1 tbsp cornflour

3 tbsp cold water

1 tbsp freshly chopped mint

1 tbsp freshly chopped basil

CLAMS *with* CHILLI *and* HERBS

Put the clams into a large bowl, cover with cold water and set aside in a cool place.

Heat the oil in a wok or large pan and sauté the onion, chillies, zested lime, ginger and garlic for 2 minutes. Add the fish sauce, coconut milk and stock. Drain the clams and add to the pan. Bring to the boil, then cover the pan and reduce the heat. Simmer for 3–5 minutes, shaking the pan or stirring occasionally.

Blend the cornflour with the water and add to the pan with the herbs. Cook, stirring, until the stock thickens. Discard any clams that have not opened and serve.

PRAWNS *with* PUMPKIN SEEDS

Camarones en pepitas

Serves 4

100 g/4 oz pumpkin seeds

1 small onion, chopped

6 tomatoes, peeled, deseeded
   and chopped

2 green jalapeño chillies

2 tbsp clear honey

300 ml/½ pt fish or vegetable stock

1 tbsp freshly chopped coriander

salt and black pepper

2 tbsp tomato purée, blended
   with 4 tbsp water

450 g/1 lb raw tiger prawns,
   thawed if frozen, peeled, tails left
   intact and deveined

fresh coriander sprigs, to garnish

freshly cooked rice or warm
   bread, to serve

Pumpkin seeds are widely used in Mexican cookery, nearly always toasted, then ground to a powder.

🌶 Preheat the grill to moderate and spread the pumpkin seeds over a grill pan. Toast for 2–3 minutes, stirring frequently to prevent them from burning. Remove from the grill and allow to cool.

🌶 Put the toasted seeds into a food processor and grind finely. Alternatively, pound in a pestle and mortar. Put the remaining ingredients, except the tomato purée and prawns, into the food processor and blend together.

🌶 Put the blended ingredients with the tomato purée into a pan and bring to a gentle boil. Reduce the heat and add the prawns. Heat through gently for 3–5 minutes, or until the prawns are cooked. Do not allow the mixture to boil, otherwise the prawns will become tough. Garnish with sprigs of coriander and serve immediately with freshly cooked rice or warm bread.

MIXED FISH CREOLE STYLE

Serves 4

2 tbsp oil

1 large onion, chopped

2 garlic cloves, crushed

4–5 rocotillo chilli peppers, deseeded

2 celery sticks, trimmed and chopped

1 red pepper, deseeded and sliced

1 green pepper, deseeded and sliced

2 tbsp tomato purée

2 tbsp water

300 ml/½ pt fish or chicken stock

400 g/14 oz can chopped tomatoes

1 tsp Worcestershire sauce

salt and pepper

225 g/8 oz white fish fillets, such as
   hoki, pollack or cod

225 g/8 oz mackerel fillets

1 tbsp freshly chopped oregano

1 tbsp freshly chopped marjoram

juice of ½ lime

100 g/4 oz peeled prawns

sprigs of fresh oregano or marjoram,
   to garnish

freshly cooked rice and green
   salad, to serve

🌶 Heat the oil in a large pan and sauté the onion, garlic, chillies and celery for 5 minutes, or until softened. Add the peppers and cook for a further 3 minutes.

🌶 Blend the tomato purée with the water and stir into the pan with the stock, chopped tomatoes, Worcestershire sauce and seasoning to taste. Bring to the boil, then reduce the heat and simmer for about 20 minutes, or until the sauce has reduced and is thick.

🌶 Skin the fish fillets and discard any bones. Cut the fish into bite-sized pieces. Rinse and pat dry with paper towels.

🌶 Add the fish with the herbs and lime juice to the pan and simmer for a further 6 minutes. Add the prawns and cook for a further 4 minutes, or until the fish is cooked. Garnish with the herbs and serve with freshly cooked rice and a tossed green salad.

CURRIED COD *with* CHILLI PEPPERS

*If liked, the dried chillies can be replaced
with 3–4 fresno chillies.*

❧ Remove any bones from the fish. Rinse, pat
dry with paper towels and cut into cubes.
❧ Heat the oil in a large pan and sauté the
onion, garlic and chillies for 5 minutes, or until
softened. Add the spices and sauté gently for a
further 5 minutes, stirring occasionally.

❧ Add the canned tomatoes, tomato purée,
water and lemon juice, and bring to the boil.
Reduce the heat and simmer for 15 minutes.
❧ Add the fish and continue cooking for
10 minutes, or until the fish is cooked. Stir in
the chopped coriander and serve with freshly
cooked rice and accompaniments.

SQUID *with* HOT PEPPER SAUCE

❧ Prepare the squid by cutting off the
tentacles and rinsing. Remove the discard the
head, innards and central transparent quill.
Rub off the purplish outer skin, rinse and slice.
❧ Put the shallots, garlic and both types of
chillies into a pestle and mortar and grind
to a paste.
❧ Heat the oil in a wok or large pan and
gently sauté the paste for 3 minutes. Add
the tomatoes, lime juice and sugar, and
cook for 10–12 minutes, or until a thick
sauce is formed.

❧ Add the oregano, reserving a little for
garnish, and squid, and simmer for 5 minutes,
or until the squid is cooked. Take care not to
overcook, otherwise the squid will become
rubbery. Serve sprinkled with the remaining
oregano. If liked, Hot Pepper Sauce (page 10)
can be added to increase the heat intensity.

Squid with Hot Pepper Sauce ▶

HEAT 4

Serves 4

675 g/1½ lb assorted white fish,
*   such as monkfish, cod and sole,*
*   cleaned and filleted*
250 ml/8 fl oz lime juice
3 tbsp olive or sunflower oil
2 onions, thinly sliced
2 garlic cloves, crushed
4 green de agua chillies, deseeded
*   and sliced*
4 tomatoes, peeled, deseeded
*   and chopped*
salt and pepper
dash of Tabasco sauce
2 tbsp freshly chopped coriander
shredded crisp lettuce
freshly chopped coriander, green pitted
*   olives and lime wedges, to garnish*
warm pitta bread or crusty
*   bread, to serve*

CEBICHE

A traditional Mexican dish, sometimes spelt seviche or, in Spain, escabèche. It can be made with just shellfish or a mixture of white and shellfish. The fish must be absolutely fresh.

🌶 Remove any bones from the fish, rinse and pat dry with paper towels. Cut into small bite-sized pieces and place in a shallow glass dish.

🌶 Pour over the lime juice, ensuring that the fish is completely covered with the juice; if necessary add extra juice. Stir, then cover the dish and leave in the refrigerator to marinate for 10–12 hours. Stir occasionally during this time. The fish is ready when the flesh is firm in texture and white.

🌶 Drain the juice from the fish and reserve the fish. Mix the remaining ingredients together, except the lettuce and garnishes. Stir in the drained fish.

🌶 Place the lettuce in a serving bowl and arrange the fish and sauce on top. Garnish and serve with warm pitta bread or crusty bread.

MEXICAN CRAB

Jaiba Mexicana

HEAT 4-5

Serves 4

1 tbsp corn or sunflower oil
1 onion, finely chopped
1 garlic clove, crushed
2 green New Mexico chillies, deseeded
*   and finely chopped*
2 cooked crabs, inedible parts
*   discarded and flaked or 350 g/12 oz*
*   flaked white crab meat*
50 g/2 oz fresh white breadcrumbs
50 g/2 oz sweetcorn kernels
2 (size 3) eggs, hard-boiled, shelled
*   and finely chopped*
salt and pepper
1 tbsp freshly chopped parsley
zested rind of 1 lime
lime twists and fresh herbs, to garnish

🌶 Preheat the oven to 180°C/350°F/Gas Mark 4.

🌶 Heat the oil in a large pan and gently sauté the onion, garlic and chillies for 5 minutes, or until softened. Remove from the heat and stir in the crab meat.

🌶 Stir in half the breadcrumbs, the sweetcorn kernels, chopped egg, seasoning to taste, parsley and lime zest. Mix together well.

🌶 Divide the mixture between four cleaned crab shells or individual ovenproof dishes and sprinkle with the remaining breadcrumbs. Bake for 20 minutes, or until thoroughly heated through. Garnish with lime twists and fresh herbs.

◄ *Cebiche*

HEAT 4–5

Serves 4

Salsa

175 g/6 oz ripe tomatoes, peeled
   and deseeded

2 shallots, finely chopped

2 green de agua chillies, roasted,
   peeled, deseeded and finely chopped

1 small green pepper, roasted, peeled,
   deseeded and finely chopped

1–2 tsp molasses sugar

1 small ripe papaya, peeled, stone
   removed and finely chopped

Tuna

4 tuna steaks, about 175 g/6 oz each

2 tbsp olive oil

juice of 2 limes

salt and pepper

fresh flat-leaf parsley to garnish

freshly toasted bread, such as ciabatta,
   drizzled with olive oil, to serve

HEAT 5–6

Serves 4

450 g/1 lb fish fillets, such as
mackerel, sea bream, bass or pollack

1 tbsp corn or sunflower oil

1 large onion, sliced

5 red serrano chillies, deseeded and
   sliced thinly

1 tsp ground ginger

1 tsp ground cinnamon

1 tsp ground cumin

3 carrots, sliced

675 g/1½ lb potatoes, peeled and
   thickly sliced

600 ml/1 pt fish or vegetable stock

2 courgettes, trimmed and sliced

salt and pepper

100 g/4 oz raw prawns, peeled

2 tbsp freshly chopped tarragon

warm bread, to serve

GRILLED TUNA
with PAPAYA SALSA

⤖ Mix the salsa ingredients together. Put into a bowl, cover and leave for at least 1 hour for the flavours to develop.

⤖ Preheat the grill to medium and line the grill rack with foil. Wipe the tuna steaks and pat dry with paper towels. Mix the oil and lime juice with seasoning to taste and brush over both sides of the tuna steaks.

⤖ Place the fish on the foil-lined rack and cook under the grill for 2 minutes on each side. Reduce the heat and grill for a further 3 minutes on each side, or until the fish is cooked. Serve on the toasted bread with the salsa. Garnish with parsley and lemon wedges.

SPICY FISH STEW

⤖ Remove any bones from the fish, then rinse and pat dry with paper towels. Cut into small cubes.

⤖ Heat the oil in a large pan and sauté the onion and chillies for 5 minutes. Add the spices and cook for a further 3 minutes.

⤖ Add the carrots, potatoes and stock. Bring to the boil, cover the pan, reduce the heat and simmer gently for 15 minutes, or until the potatoes are beginning to break down.

⤖ Add the courgettes, cubed fish and the prawns, and cook for 5–8 minutes, or until the vegetables and fish are cooked. Season to taste and stir in the chopped tarragon. Serve in deep bowls with warm bread.

Grilled Tuna with Papaya Salsa ▶

Serves 4

2 large red mullet or snappers,
    filleted and boned

4 tbsp olive oil

120 ml/4 fl oz lime juice

2 green Anaheim chillies, deseeded
    and finely sliced

1–2 tsp Mexican honey, warmed

Tomato Coulis

1 tbsp olive oil

2 shallots, chopped

1 garlic clove, crushed

3 red Anaheim chillies, deseeded
    and chopped

1 tbsp tomato purée

1 tbsp water

450 g/1 lb ripe tomatoes, peeled,
    deseeded and chopped

juice of ½ lemon

salt and pepper

a few sprigs of watercress, lime
    wedges and zested lime rind,
    to garnish

RED MULLET *with*
TOMATO COULIS

Rinse the fish and pat dry with paper towels. Place in a shallow dish. Mix the oil, lime juice, chillies and honey together and pour over the fish. Cover and leave to marinate for at least 1 hour. Turn occasionally during this time.

Meanwhile, make the coulis. Heat the oil in a pan and sauté the shallots, garlic and chillies for 5 minutes, or until softened. Blend the tomato purée with the water and add to the pan, together with the chopped tomatoes, lime juice and seasoning. Bring to the boil, cover the pan, reduce the heat and simmer for 15 minutes.

Remove from the heat and allow to cool slightly. Purée in a food processor. Then pass through a fine sieve to remove any seeds. Check the seasoning and heat gently when required.

Preheat the grill to medium and line the grill rack with foil. Drain the fish and place on the foil-lined grill rack. Cook for 8–10 minutes, or until cooked. Turn the fish once during cooking.

To serve, pour the tomato coulis on to four serving plates and place the cooked fish on top. Garnish with watercress, lime wedges and zested lime rind.

HEAT 5

Serves 4

8–12 fresh sardines (depending
   on size), cleaned
120 ml/4 fl oz orange juice
4 tbsp olive oil
4 green jalapeño chillies, deseeded
   and finely sliced
1 tbsp soft brown sugar
few sprigs of fresh rosemary
orange wedges and sprigs of fresh
   rosemary, to garnish

ORANGE *and* CHILLI MARINATED SARDINES

✎ Wipe or lightly rinse the sardines and pat dry with paper towels. Place in a shallow dish. Mix the orange juice, oil, chillies and sugar together and pour over the sardines. Tear the sprigs of rosemary into small pieces and scatter over the top. Cover and chill for at least 2 hours, turning the sardines occasionally.

✎ Preheat the grill to medium and line the grill rack with foil. Drain the sardines and place on the foil-lined grill rack. Cook under the grill for 3–4 minutes, or until cooked, basting with the marinade at least once during cooking. Garnish with orange wedges and sprigs of rosemary.

✎ If liked, the sardines could be cooked on a barbecue for about 3–4 minutes once the coals are ready. It is best to place them in a hinged fish rack.

HEAT 5

Serves 4

4 haddock or cod steaks, about
   175 g/6 oz each
1 tbsp corn or sunflower oil
2 garlic cloves, crushed
3 red jalapeño chillies, deseeded
   and finely sliced
1 tsp turmeric
1 tsp ground cumin
1 tsp ground coriander
1 tsp ground fenugreek
6 cardamom pods, crushed
150 ml/¼ pt natural yogurt
25 g/1 oz toasted flaked almonds
fresh herbs, to garnish

YOGURT SPICED FISH

✎ Lightly rinse the fish, cut into cubes and place in a shallow dish.

✎ Heat the oil and gently sauté the garlic and chillies for 3 minutes, stirring frequently. Add the spices and cook gently for a further 3–4 minutes. Remove from the heat and stir in the yogurt. Pour over the fish, then cover and leave to marinate in the refrigerator for at least 1 hour, turning the fish over after 30 minutes.

✎ Preheat the grill to medium and line the grill rack with foil. Drain the fish from the yogurt mixture and thread on to skewers. Cook under the grill for 3–4 minutes, or until cooked. Serve sprinkled with the almonds and garnished with fresh herbs.

Orange and Chilli ▶
Marinated Sardines

BARBECUED KING PRAWNS

HEAT 4-5

Serves 4

*450 g/1 lb raw tiger prawns,
thawed if frozen*
salad leaves and lime twists, to garnish

Marinade
grated rind and juice of 2 limes
*3 huachinango chillies, deseeded
and sliced*
*2 lemon grass stalks, outer leaves
removed and sliced*
*5 cm/2 in piece root ginger, peeled
and grated*
2 garlic cloves, crushed
1 tbsp clear honey, warmed
6 tbsp olive oil
1 tbsp freshly chopped coriander

❧ If using fresh prawns, peel and devein. Place in a shallow dish. Mix the marinade ingredients together and pour over the prawns. Cover and leave to marinate for at least 4 hours, turning occasionally in the marinade.

❧ Preheat the grill to moderately hot or light the barbecue coals 20 minutes before required.

❧ Have ready four long wooden skewers that have been soaked in cold water for 1 hour.

Drain the prawns and reserve a little of the marinade. Thread the prawns on to the skewers and brush with the marinade.

❧ Cook under the grill, or on the barbecue, turning at least once, for 5 minutes, or until cooked. Serve garnished with salad leaves and lime twists.

SCALLOPS *with* HABANERO *and* MANGO SALSA

HEAT 8–9

Serves 4

Salsa
*1 small ripe mango, peeled, stone
removed and finely chopped*
*3 spring onions, trimmed and
finely chopped*
*2 orange habanero chillies, deseeded
and chopped*
*5 cm/2 in piece cucumber, deseeded
and finely diced*
*2 tomatoes, peeled, deseeded and
finely chopped*
1–2 tsp dark brown or molasses sugar
2 tbsp freshly chopped chervil

Scallops
12 large fresh scallops, cleaned
50 g/2 oz unsalted butter
1 tbsp olive or sunflower oil
*assorted bitter salad leaves such as
rocket, escarole, radicchio and
chicory*
edible flowers, to garnish

❧ Combine all the salsa ingredients together, put into a bowl and cover. Chill for 15 minutes and then use immediately.

❧ Cut the scallops into thick slices. Rinse and thoroughly dry. Heat the butter and oil in a frying pan. When the butter is bubbling slightly, add the scallops and cook gently for 2–3 minutes, or until just cooked. Drain.

❧ Arrange the salad leaves on a serving platter or in a bowl and top with the scallops. Garnish with the edible flowers and serve with the salsa.

◄ *Barbecued King Prawns*

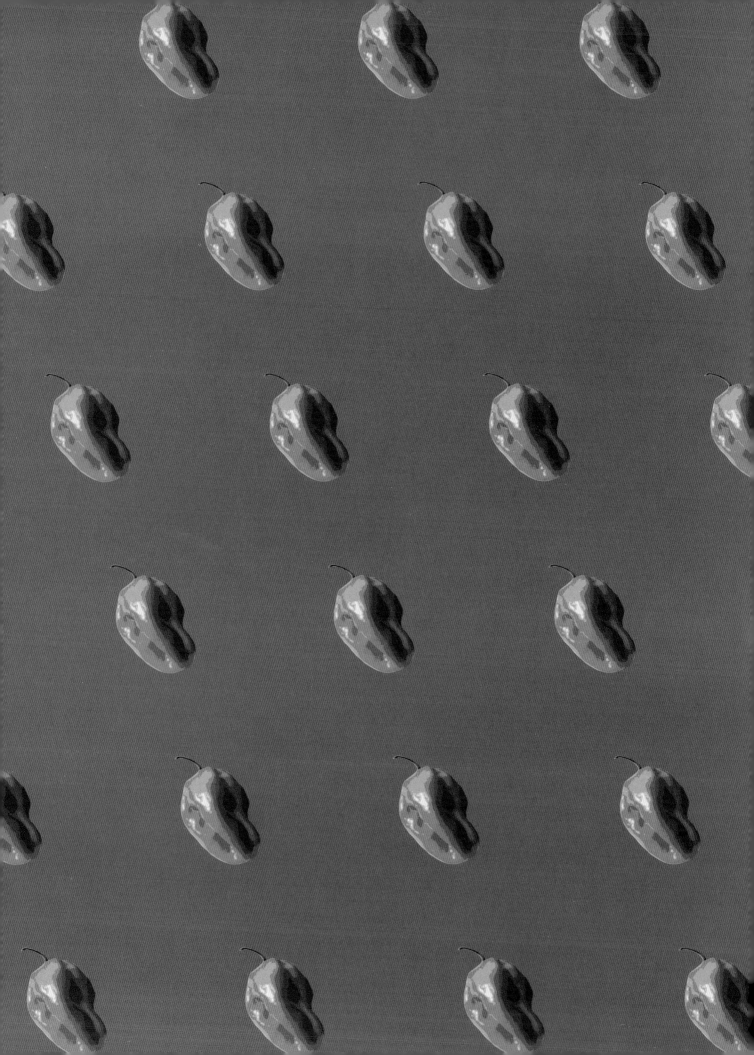

Chapter 6

Poultry

DUCK *in* GREEN CHILLI SAUCE

HEAT 5

Serves 4

4 green serrano chillies, deseeded
  and sliced

225 g/8 oz tomatillos or green
  tomatoes, deseeded and chopped

1 onion, chopped

2 garlic cloves, chopped

grated rind of ½ lemon, if using
  green tomatoes

150 ml/¼ pt chicken stock

2 tbsp freshly chopped coriander

2 tsp clear honey

salt and pepper

1 tbsp arrowroot

1 tbsp water

4 duck breasts

Salsa Rojo (page 46), to serve

coriander sprigs to garnish

Tomatillos are a type of tomato with a zesty bitter flavour that have a papery husk around each fruit. When cooked they lose their bitterness but still retain their lemony tang. They can also be bought canned.

❧ Preheat the grill to moderately high.

❧ Put the chillies, tomatillos or tomatoes, onion, garlic and lemon rind, if using, into a food processor and blend to form a purée. Push through a fine sieve into a pan and gradually stir in the stock.

❧ Heat the chilli mixture gently for 4 minutes, stirring occasionally. Then stir in the coriander, honey and seasoning to taste.

Blend the arrowroot with the water, stir into the pan and cook, stirring constantly, until the sauce thickens and clears. Keep warm.

❧ Wipe the duck breasts, discard any excess fat and prick the skin with a fork. Season with salt and pepper.

❧ Place the duck breasts, skin side uppermost, in a grill pan and cook, turning at least once, for 25 minutes, or until cooked to personal preference.

❧ To serve, pour a little of the chilli sauce on to each serving plate and slice the duck breasts. Arrange in a fan shape with the Salsa Rojo and serve extra sauce separately. Garnish with coriander sprigs.

CHILLI CHICKEN *with* PINE NUTS

HEAT 6

Serves 4

1 tbsp sunflower oil

1 tbsp butter

4 chicken portions

100 g/4 oz lean bacon, trimmed
  and cubed

1 onion, sliced

1 garlic clove, crushed

4 green fresno chillies, deseeded
  and sliced

25 g/1 oz plain flour

450 ml/¾ pt chicken stock

grated rind of 1 lemon

salt and pepper

100 g/4 oz sweetcorn kernels

2 tbsp freshly chopped parsley

3 tbsp pine kernels (nuts), toasted

❧ Preheat the oven to 190°C/375°F/Gas Mark 5.

❧ Heat the oil and butter in a frying pan and seal the chicken portions and bacon on all sides. Drain and place in a large ovenproof casserole.

❧ Add the onion, garlic and chillies to the frying pan and gently sauté for 5 minutes, or until softened. Sprinkle in the flour and cook, stirring constantly for 2 minutes. Gradually add the stock, then bring to the boil. Add the lemon rind with seasoning to taste.

❧ Pour the onion mixture over the chicken, cover the casserole and cook for 40 minutes. Remove from the oven and stir in the sweetcorn. Cook for a further 15 minutes or until the chicken portions are cooked. Stir in the parsley and pine kernels, and serve.

Duck in Green Chilli Sauce ▶

HEAT 7

Serves 4

*300 g/10 oz boneless chicken
  breasts, skinned*

Marinade
2 shallots, finely chopped
1 garlic clove, crushed
*4 Thai red chillies, deseeded
  and chopped*
*5 cm/2 in piece root ginger, peeled
  and grated*
2 tbsp soy sauce
2 tsp clear honey, warmed
2 tbsp lemon juice
chopped chilli to garnish

Nuoc Cham
*1 Thai red chilli, deseeded and
  finely chopped*
1 tbsp lime juice
50 ml/2 fl oz Thai fish sauce
1 tbsp roasted peanuts, finely crushed
*2 spring onions, trimmed and
  finely shredded*

CHICKEN STRIPS *with*
NUOC CHAM

*Nuoc Cham is a traditional Vietnamese
dipping sauce served at the table to season
dishes. The sauce can also be stirred into
soups and rice dishes, or poured over fish
and meat dishes.*

❧ Cut the chicken breasts into narrow strips, about 7.5 x 1.25 cm 3 x ½ in, and place in a shallow dish. Combine all the marinade ingredients together and pour over the chicken strips. Turn to ensure they are well coated. Cover the dish and chill for at least 3 hours, turning the chicken occasionally in the marinade.

❧ Preheat the grill to moderately high.

❧ Drain the chicken and thread on to wooden skewers that have been soaked in cold water for 1 hour.

❧ Meanwhile, prepare the Nuoc Cham sauce. Put all the ingredients into a small pan and heat through, stirring occasionally. Reserve.

❧ Brush the chicken strips with a little of the marinade and grill, brushing occasionally with the marinade and turning the strips, for 8–10 minutes, or until cooked. Serve with the sauce, garnished with the chopped chilli.

HEAT 7

Serves 6

3 tbsp sunflower or olive oil

25 g/1 oz plain flour

5 ancho dried chillies, roasted and
  rehydrated (page 16)

1 garlic clove, crushed

3 shallots, chopped

2 tbsp tomato purée

200 ml/7 fl oz chicken stock

1 tbsp freshly chopped oregano

350 g/12 oz cooked chicken meat,
  cut into thin strips

100 g/4 oz sweetcorn kernels

1 litre/1¾ pts water

300 g/10 oz cornmeal or polenta

2 tsp chilli powder

1–2 tsp salt

1 tsp pepper

2 tbsp olive oil

Salsa Rojo (page 46) and green
  salad, to serve

HEAT 5

Serves 4

120 ml/4 fl oz white wine vinegar

½ tsp ground cloves

1 tsp ground cinnamon

2 tsp juniper berries, crushed

4 tbsp olive or sunflower oil

1 onion, chopped

3 garlic cloves, crushed

100 g/4 oz dark brown sugar

6 smoked dried chillies, such as
  Pailla de Oaxaco or Chipotle Grande,
  roasted, rehydrated (page 16) and
  chopped

2 tbsp tomato purée

150 ml/¼ pt water

1 tsp Worcestershire sauce

8 turkey thighs

sliced starfruit and salad leaves
  to garnish

rice salad, to serve

TAMALE PIE

This is one of Mexico's oldest dishes, dating back to Aztec times and traditionally served at festivals and feast days. It is rather like a stuffed dumpling – the dough is wrapped in corn husks, then steamed and served with a salsa or mole sauce.

➤ Heat the sunflower or olive oil in a pan, add the flour and cook, very gently, stirring frequently, for 8–10 minutes, or until browned. Take great care not to burn the mixture.

➤ Chop the rehydrated chillies and add to the flour mixture with the garlic, shallots, tomato purée blended with the stock, and the oregano. Bring to the boil, then reduce the heat and simmer for 15 minutes. Add the chicken and sweetcorn, mix well and set aside until cool.

➤ Bring the water to just below boiling point, then take off the heat and gradually stir in the cornmeal or polenta, chilli powder, salt and pepper in a thin steady stream. Stir until smooth, then return to a moderate heat and simmer for 5–10 minutes, stirring occasionally.

➤ Preheat the oven to 180°C/350°F/Gas Mark 4.

➤ Spread half the cornmeal or polenta mixture in the base of a lightly oiled 20 cm/8 in oblong ovenproof dish and place the cooled chicken mixture on top. Cover with the remaining cornmeal mixture. Drizzle with the 2 tbsp of olive oil. Bake for about 1 hour, or until the top is golden brown. Serve cut into wedges with Salsa Rojo and green salad.

TURKEY *with* SMOKED CHILLI BARBECUE SAUCE

Most barbecue sauces are made with cayenne and other hot chillies. The use of dried chillies in this sauce gives it a roundness or smoothness that you would not get with just fresh chillies. If however dried are unavailable, fresno chillies will make a delicious and appetizing sauce.

➤ Put the vinegar in a pan with the spices and bring to the boil. Boil for 3 minutes and set aside.

➤ Heat the oil in a frying pan and sauté the onion and garlic for 5 minutes, or until softened. Add the sugar and boil for 3 minutes. Then stir in the vinegar mixture, chopped chillies, tomato purée, water and

Worcestershire sauce. Cook over a gentle heat for about 30 minutes and allow to cool slightly before using.

➤ Place the turkey thighs in a shallow dish and pour over the sauce. Cover the dish and leave to chill for at least 2 hours, turning the turkey at least once during the marinading.

➤ Preheat the grill to moderate.

➤ Drain the turkey and place on a foil-lined grill rack. Brush with a little of the marinade. Cook under the grill for 12-15 minutes, brushing with the marinade and turning occasionally, until the turkey is cooked. Serve, garnished with sliced starfruit, salad leaves and a rice salad.

Turkey with Smoked Chilli ▶
Barbecue Sauce

ARROZ CON POLLO

Serves 4

3 tbsp olive or sunflower oil

4 chicken portions, cut in half

1 Spanish onion, chopped

2 garlic cloves, crushed

5 red Anaheim chillies, deseeded
  and sliced

225 g/8 oz risotto rice

few strands of saffron

600–900 ml/1–1½ pt chicken stock

salt and pepper

100 g/4 oz peeled raw prawns

100 g/4 oz peas

100 g/4 oz green beans,
  trimmed and sliced

450 g/1 lb fresh mussels, scrubbed,
  beards removed and any open
  ones discarded

lemon wedges and flat-leaf
  parsley, to garnish

If using cooked prawns, add at the end of cooking time when the chicken is cooked and heat through for 2–3 minutes.

❧ Heat the oil in a paella or large frying pan and brown the chicken on all sides. Remove from the pan and drain on paper towels.

❧ Add the onion, garlic and chillies to the pan and sauté for 5 minutes. Add the rice and saffron, and cook, stirring occasionally for a further 3 minutes.

❧ Return the chicken to the pan and stir in 450 ml/¾ pt of the stock and seasoning. Bring to the boil, then simmer for 20 minutes, adding more stock as necessary.

❧ Add the prawns, vegetables and mussels to the pan with extra stock as required and cook for a further 8–10 minutes, or until the rice and chicken are cooked. Discard any mussels that have not opened. Season to taste and serve garnished with lemon wedges and parsley.

SIZZLING CHICKEN FAJITAS

Serves 4

2 tbsp sunflower oil

225 g/8 oz boneless chicken breasts,
  cut into thin strips

1 onion, cut into wedges

2 garlic cloves

4 red fresno chillies, deseeded
  and sliced

1 red pepper, deseeded and
  cut into strips

1 green pepper, deseeded and
  cut into strips

2 courgettes, trimmed and
  cut into strips

8 wheat tortillas, warmed

150 ml/¼ pt soured cream

Guacamole (page 29)

1 bunch spring onions, trimmed and
  cut into strips

7.5 cm/3 in piece cucumber, trimmed
  and cut into thin strips

Ready-made fajitas marinades are available but it is well worth making your own as you can then vary the flavour according to the ingredients you use. Fajitas can be made from seafood, pork and just vegetables, as well as beef and chicken. They are best served in warm tortillas with spicy salsas and soured cream.

❧ Heat the oil in a heavy-based pan and cook the chicken strips over a high heat stirring constantly, for 5 minutes, or until cooked. Drain and reserve.

❧ Add the onion, garlic and chillies to the oil in the pan over a high heat for 2 minutes. Add the peppers and courgettes, and cook over a high heat for 4 minutes, or until the vegetables have begun to blacken very slightly at the edges.

❧ Return the chicken to the pan and heat until piping hot. Serve immediately. Spread a warmed tortilla with soured cream and Guacamole, top with some chicken and vegetable mixture, spring onions and cucumber. Roll up and eat.

◀ *Arroz con Pollo*

TURKEY *in* CHOCOLATE SAUCE

Mole Poblano

Serves 4

3 dried ancho chillies

3 dried pasilla chillies

3 dried mulato chillies

I onion, sliced

2 garlic cloves, crushed

25 g/I oz sesame seeds, toasted

25 g/I oz blanched almonds, cut into slivers and toasted

I tsp ground coriander

½ tsp freshly ground black pepper

few cloves

3–4 tbsp sunflower oil

300 ml/½ pt chicken stock

450 g/I lb tomatoes, peeled, deseeded and chopped

2 tsp ground cinnamon

50 g/2 oz raisins

50 g/2 oz pumpkin seeds, toasted

50 g/2 oz dark chocolate, melted

I tbsp red wine vinegar

8 turkey thigh portions or 4 boneless chicken breasts

extra sesame seeds, toasted, and fresh herbs, to garnish

To many the idea of adding chocolate to a savoury dish may seem a little strange but Mexican chocolate is bitter, not at all like the chocolate we know. Use the darkest unsweetened chocolate you can find. Chicken is everyday fare in Mexico, while turkey is kept for festivals and special occasions. If the dried chillies are unavailable, use the darkest chilli powder you can find.

Roast the dried chillies and rehydrate as described on page 16 and put into a food processor or a pestle and mortar with the onion, garlic, sesame seeds, almonds, coriander, black pepper and cloves. Grind to form a paste.

Heat 2 tbsp of the oil in a heavy-based pan and gently sauté the paste for 5 minutes, stirring frequently.

Add 150 ml/¼ pt of the stock, the tomatoes, cinnamon, raisins and pumpkin seeds. Bring to the boil, then reduce the heat and simmer for 15 minutes, or until a thick consistency is reached. Stir in the melted chcolate and vinegar, mixing together well, cover, keep warm and reserve.

Meanwhile, heat the remaining oil in a frying pan and seal the turkey thighs or chicken breasts on all sides. Drain off the oil and add the remaining stock. Bring to the boil, then reduce the heat and simmer for 15 minutes, or until tender and drain off any liquor.

Pour the sauce over the turkey or chicken and reheat gently. Serve garnished with roasted sesame seeds and fresh herbs.

Turkey in Chocolate Sauce ▶

BARBECUED CHICKEN WINGS

HEAT 5

Serves 4

12–16 chicken wings

Salsa Verde (page 47), tossed green
*   salad and warm bread, to serve*

Marinade

2 tbsp sunflower oil

2 tbsp dark soft brown sugar

2 tbsp soy sauce

120 ml/4 fl oz orange juice

2 garlic cloves, crushed

4 red jalapeño chillies, deseeded
*   and sliced*

Wipe the chicken wings and trim if necessary. Place in a large shallow dish.

Mix all the marinade ingredients together in a pan and heat through, stirring occasionally, until the sugar has dissolved. Bring to the boil and boil for 5 minutes. Allow to cool slightly, then pour over the chicken wings. Turn the wings to ensure they are well coated, then cover the dish and leave in a cool place for at least 3 hours. Turn the wings or spoon the marinade over the chicken occasionally.

Preheat the grill to moderately hot. Alternatively, light barbecue coals 20 minutes before cooking.

Drain the chicken wings, reserving a little of the marinade, and thread on to wooden skewers that have been soaked in cold water for 1 hour. Place on a grill rack lined with foil or over the barbecue coals and brush with the reserved marinade. Cook, turning occasionally and brushing with the reserved marinade, for 10–12 minutes, or until the wings are cooked. Serve with the Salsa Verde, salad and bread.

TURKEY TAMALES

HEAT 5

Serves 4

Tamales

8 dried corn husks

200 g/7 oz white vegetable fat or lard

450 g/1 lb masa harina or
*   polenta, sifted*

1 tsp baking powder

1 tsp salt

about 450 ml/¾ pt chicken
*   stock, warmed*

Filling

2 tbsp sunflower oil

1 onion, chopped

3 garlic cloves, crushed

5 red de agua chillies, deseeded
*   and chopped*

1 small red pepper, deseeded
*   and chopped*

1 small green pepper, deseeded
*   and chopped*

2 tbsp tomato purée

2 tbsp water

75 g/3 oz sweetcorn kernels

salt and pepper

2 tbsp chopped oregano

300 g/10 oz cooked turkey meat,
*   shredded or minced*

Salsa Verde (page 47), to serve

fresh herbs, to garnish

Masa harina is a corn flour used for making corn tortillas. The corn is treated by being boiled in lime water for several hours, then drained and dried. The outer skin is removed and the kernels ground into cornmeal. If unavailable, use polenta or yellow cornmeal.

Soak the corn husks overnight in warm water.

Cream the fat until soft and sift the dry ingredients together. Gradually beat the masa harina or polenta into the lard with a little of the stock after each addition, until a firm but pliable dough is formed. Chill while preparing the filling.

Heat the oil in a frying pan and sauté the onion, garlic and chillies for 5 minutes, or until softened. Add the red and green peppers and sauté for a further 3 minutes. Blend the tomato

purée with the water and pour into the pan with the remaining chicken stock. Bring to the boil and simmer for 5 minutes Add the sweetcorn, seasoning, oregano and turkey, and mix together well.

Drain the corn husks (alternatively, you could use oblongs of foil) and place on the work surface. Form the chilled dough into rectangular shapes a little smaller than the corn husks or foil, and place on top of the husks or foil. Divide the filling between the husks or foil and fold the long side over to encase the filling.

Place upright in a steamer over a pan of simmering water. Cover the steamer with a lid and cook for 1 hour, refilling the pan with boiling water as necessary. Serve with Salsa Verde garnished with fresh herbs.

◀ *Barbecued Chicken Wings*

VIETNAMESE GRILLED CHICKEN

HEAT 5–7

Serves 4

6 ancho dried chillies, roasted,
rehydrated (page 16) and deseeded

2 lemon grass stalks, outer leaves
removed and chopped

2 garlic cloves, crushed

5 cm/2 in piece root ginger, peeled
and grated

175 g/6 oz onions, chopped

1 tbsp dark brown sugar

1 tsp turmeric

2 tbsp sunflower oil

4 chicken portions, cut in half

flat-leaf parsley, lemon wedges and
sliced green chillies to garnish

If preferred, bird's eye (Thai) chillies can be substituted for the dried chillies. Depending on your heat tolerance, you should use 1–3 bird's eye (Thai) chillies instead of the dried ancho chillies.

✎ Put the chillies into a food processor with the lemon grass, garlic, ginger, onions, sugar and turmeric. Blend to form a thick, chunky paste.

✎ Heat the oil in a frying pan and sauté the paste, stirring constantly, for 2 minutes. Remove from the heat, allow to cool slightly and brush over the chicken portions. Cover the chicken and leave in a cool place for at least 3 hours.

✎ Preheat the grill to moderately hot.

✎ Place the chicken on a grill rack lined with foil and cook, turning occasionally, for 15 minutes, or until the chicken is cooked. Serve garnished with flat-leaf parsley, lemon wedges and slices of green chillies.

DUCK BREASTS
with PIPIAN VERDE

HEAT 5

Serves 4

Pipián Verde

50 g/2 oz pumpkin seeds, toasted

2 tbsp sunflower oil

1 small onion, chopped

3–4 green fresno chillies, deseeded
and chopped

2 garlic cloves, chopped

150 ml/¼ pt chicken stock

1 tbsp freshly chopped coriander

¼ tsp salt

100 g/4 oz fresh spinach leaves,
prepared and chopped

4 duck breasts, about 175 g/6 oz each

This sauce contains pumpkin seeds which are used to thicken and flavour. Mexicans also use sesame seeds and pine kernels. Toasted pumpkin seeds can also be used as appetizers with drinks.

✎ Reserve a few of the pumpkin seeds for garnish and finely grind the remainder.

✎ Heat the oil in a pan and gently sauté the onion, chillies and garlic for 3 minutes. Add the stock and simmer for 1 minute. Add the ground pumpkin seeds, coriander, salt and spinach to the pan and simmer for a further 3 minutes. Remove from the heat and keep warm.

✎ Preheat the grill to high.

✎ Meanwhile, prick the skin on the duck breasts with a fork and place, skin-side uppermost, in a foil–lined grill pan. Cook under the grill for 2 minutes, on both sides, then with skin sides uppermost, reduce the grill to moderately hot and continue grilling, for 15–20 minutes turning at least once, or according to personal preference. Serve the duck breasts, sprinkled with the reserved pumpkin seeds, with the Pipián Verde.

Vietnamese Grilled Chicken ▶

ROASTED DUCK
with CHILLI

HEAT 4-5

Serves 4

1 x 1.75 kg/4 lb oven-ready duck

4 red serrano chillies, deseeded and
  finely chopped

2 tbsp dark brown sugar

1 tsp salt

1 tsp ground cinnamon

½ tsp ground cloves

zested rind of 1 lime

zested lime rind and flat-leaf
  parsley to garnish

Salsa

225 g/8 oz ripe tomatoes, peeled,
  deseeded and finely chopped

6 spring onions, trimmed and
  finely chopped

1 Grenadillo, halved, with
  seeds removed

2 red serrano chillies, deseeded
  and finely chopped

Wipe the duck, inside and out, discarding any excess fat from the cavity. Prick the skin all over with a fork. Mix the chillies, sugar, salt, cinnamon, cloves and lime zest together. Sprinkle the inside of the duck with 1 tbsp of the mixture and use the remainder to rub all over the duck skin. Leave in a cool place for at least 4 hours.

Preheat the oven to 200°C/400°F/Gas Mark 6 15 minutes before roasting the duck.

Place the duck on a trivet or rack standing in a roasting tin. Roast in the oven for 1¾–2 hours, or until the duck is cooked.

Meanwhile, make the Salsa. Combine all the ingredients and leave for at least 30 minutes to allow the flavours to develop. Serve with the cooked duck, garnished with lime rind and flat-leaf parsley.

CHICKEN *in* RED CHILLI *and*
TOMATO SAUCE

HEAT 7

Serves 4

1.25 kg/2½ lb chicken

2 onions

1 carrot, roughly chopped

3 bay leaves

6 dried ancho chillies, roasted,
  rehydrated (page 16) and deseeded

2 garlic cloves

50 g/2 oz sesame seeds, toasted

½ tsp ground cinnamon

½ tsp ground cloves

1 tbsp sunflower oil

400 g/14 oz can chopped tomatoes

1 tbsp tomato purée

1 tbsp freshly chopped oregano

salad and warm bread, to serve

When choosing tomatoes for Mexican dishes, look for the large beef tomatoes as they are the nearest thing to Mexican tomatoes. Canned tomatoes can be used instead, but you may need to reduce the liquid in the recipe.

Rinse the chicken and place in a large pan with one of the onions, the carrot and bay leaves. Cover with cold water and bring to the boil. Skim off any scum that rises to the surface. Cover the pan with a lid and simmer for 1½ hours, or until tender.

Allow to cool, then remove the cooked chicken meat from the carcase, discarding the skin, and cut into thin strips. Reserve 300 ml/½ pt of the cooking liquor.

Put the rehydrated chillies into a food processor with the remaining onion (chopped), the garlic, sesame seeds and spices. Blend with a little of the reserved stock to make a smooth paste.

Heat the oil in a frying pan and sauté the paste gently for 2 minutes. Add the chopped tomatoes, tomato purée and remaining stock. Bring to the boil, reduce the heat and simmer for 10 minutes.

Add the chicken to the pan and simmer for a further 10–15 minutes, or until the chicken is piping hot. Serve, sprinkled with the chopped oregano, with salad and warm bread.

Roasted Duck with Chilli ▶

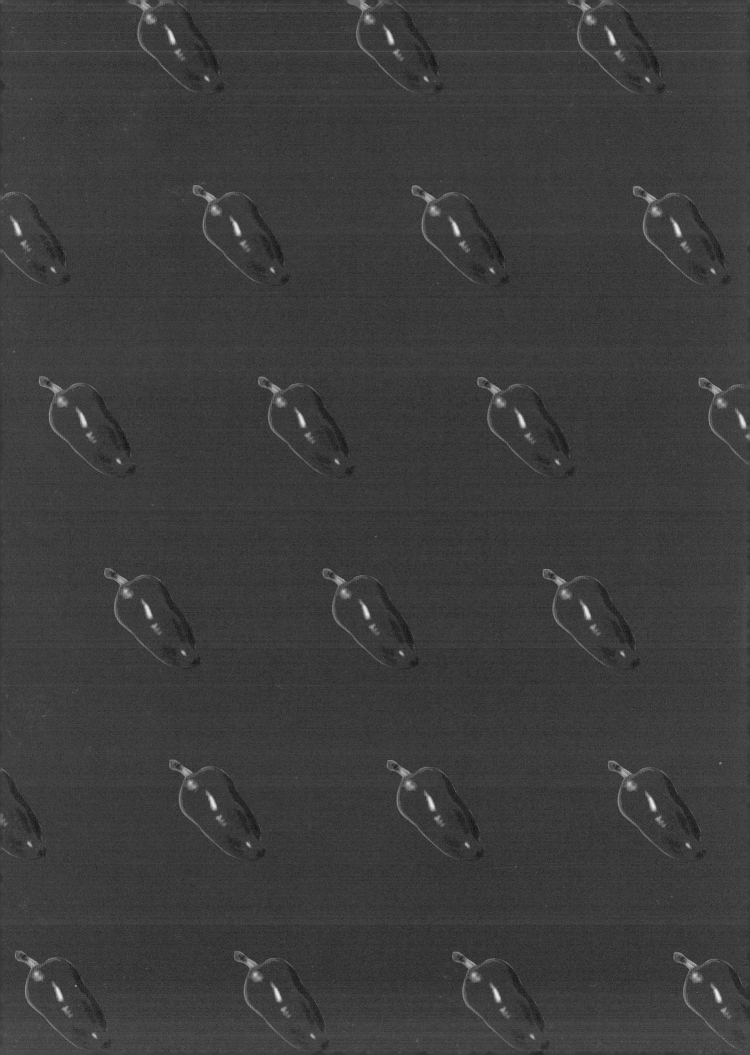

Chapter 7

Meat

HEAT 7-8

Serves 4

1 tbsp sunflower oil
1 large onion, chopped
2 garlic cloves, crushed
3 rocotillo chillies, deseeded and sliced
350 g/12 oz ground beef
1 green pepper, deseeded and
 chopped
1 tsp paprika
400 g/14 oz can chopped tomatoes
150 ml/¼ pt beef stock
1 tsp sugar
salt and pepper
400 g/14 oz can pinto or red kidney
 beans, drained and rinsed
2 tsp red wine vinegar
1 tbsp freshly chopped oregano
freshly cooked rice and soured
 cream, to serve

CHILLI CON CARNE

Perhaps the best known Mexican dish of which there are many variations, it is sometimes served with refried beans as well as rice. The soured cream helps to offset the fire from the chillies.

Heat the oil in a large pan and sauté the onion, garlic and chillies for 5 minutes, or until softened. Add the beef and cook, stirring constantly, for 5-8 minutes, or until the beef is browned and separate.

Add the green pepper and cook for 3 minutes. Then add paprika and cook for 1 minute. Add the chopped tomatoes, stock and sugar with seasoning to taste and bring to the boil. Reduce the heat and simmer for 20 minutes. Then add the drained beans and vinegar, and simmer for 10 minutes, or until the beef is cooked. Stir in the oregano and serve with the rice and soured cream.

BIRIANI

HEAT 3-4

Serves 4

3 tbsp sunflower oil or ghee
1 onion, chopped
2 garlic cloves, peeled and crushed
2.5 cm/1 in piece root ginger, peeled
 and grated
3-4 red Anaheim chillies, deseeded
 and sliced
6 green cardamom pods
1 tsp ground coriander
1 tsp ground cumin
½ tsp ground cloves
675 g/1½ lb braising steak, trimmed
 and cubed
juice of 1 lemon
2 tbsp tomato purée
3 tbsp water
750 ml/1¼ pt beef stock
150 ml/¼ pt natural yogurt
2 tbsp ground almonds
175 g/6 oz basmati rice
few strands of saffron
1 hard-boiled egg, shelled and sliced
1 tbsp pistachio nuts, chopped

Birianis were developed by the Moghul chefs who cooked for the Indian Emperors. The classic method is to part-cook the rice and filling then layer them and continue their cooking. A rich and attractive dish which needs no other accompaniments except for a couple of pickles or chutneys.

Heat the oil or ghee in a large pan and sauté the onion, garlic, ginger and chillies for 5 minutes. Add the spices and sauté for a further 3 minutes. Using a slotted spoon, remove the onion mixture from the pan and reserve.

Add half the beef to the pan and sauté for 5 minutes, or until sealed, stirring frequently. Drain and reserve. Repeat with the remaining beef. Then return the onion mixture and both batches of sealed beef to the pan.

Add the lemon juice and tomato purée blended with the water, and the stock. Bring to the boil, cover the pan, then reduce the heat and simmer gently for 1 hour, stirring occasionally. Stir in the yogurt and ground almonds.

Meanwhile, cook the rice for 10 minutes with the saffron threads in lightly salted water. Drain and reserve.

Preheat the oven to 180°C/350°F/Gas Mark 4.

Place half the rice in the base of an ovenproof dish or casserole and cover with the beef mixture. Spoon the remaining rice on top and cover with a lid or foil. Cook in the oven for about 40 minutes, or until the beef is tender. Serve garnished with the hard-boiled egg and pistachio nuts.

EMPANADAS

Serves 6

75 g/3 oz ground pork

75 g/3 oz ground beef

1 small onion, finely chopped

2 Scotch bonnet chillies, deseeded and
    finely chopped

½ small red pepper, deseeded and
    finely chopped

½ small green pepper, deseeded and
    finely chopped

½ tsp ground cloves

1 tsp ground cinnamon

1 tbsp tomato purée

5 tbsp water

1 tsp clear honey

juice of 1 lime

675 g/1½ lb prepared
    shortcrust pastry

oil for deep-frying

Red or Green Chilli Sauce (page 47)

*Empanadas are little filled pastry turnovers
that are either deep fried or baked. The filling
can be sweet or savoury. In Mexico they are
sold on stalls in the street and usually served
with a red or green chilli sauce.*

Put the pork and beef into a non-stick frying pan and cook over a gentle heat, stirring constantly, for 8 minutes, or until the meat has browned. Use the spoon to break up any lumps.

Add the onion and chillies, and cook for 5 minutes, stirring frequently. Add both the peppers and spices, and cook for a further 3 minutes. Blend the tomato purée with the water and add to the pan, together with the honey and lime juice. Bring to the boil, then simmer for 15 minutes, stirring frequently, or until most of the liquid has evaporated. Allow to cool.

Roll the pastry out on a lightly floured surface and cut out 12 10 cm/4 in circles. Divide the filling between the pastry circles, brush the edges with water and fold over to make small pasties. Pinch the edges together firmly.

Heat the oil to 180°C/350°F and fry the Empanadas, a few at a time, for 3 minutes or until golden brown. Drain on paper towels and serve with Red or Green Chilli Sauce.

HOT *and* SOUR BEEF FONDUE

Serves 4

300 ml ½ pt good quality beef stock

4 star anise

few cloves

few peppercorns

5 cm/2 in. piece root ginger, peeled and chopped

1 onion, sliced

1 garlic clove, sliced

3 Thai green chillies, deseeded and sliced

3 tbsp red wine vinegar

1 tbsp clear honey

350 g/12 oz beef fillet, trimmed and sliced into thin strips

1 red pepper, deseeded and cut into strips

1 yellow pepper, deseeded and cut into strips

2 courgettes, trimmed and cut into strips

1 fresh pineapple, peeled, cored and cut into small wedges

175 g/6 oz bean sprouts

Sauce

1 tbsp soy sauce

2 tsp fish sauce

1 tsp clear honey, warmed

1 Thai red chilli, deseeded and sliced

This recipe is based on the Mongolian Hot Pot which is their version of a cheese fondue or the French beef fondue. The food is cooked in the hot stock which is drunk at the end of the meal to clear the palate.

Put the stock into a pan with the spices, ginger, onion, garlic and chillies. Bring to the boil and simmer for 10 minutes, then add the vinegar and honey. Pour into a fondue pot placed over a burner and keep warm.

Put the beef, peppers, courgettes and pineapple wedges into individual serving bowls.

Combine the sauce ingredients and pour into small dishes.

To serve, spear the beef or vegetables on to skewers and dip into the hot stock for 1–2 minutes, or until cooked to personal preference. Dip into the sauce before eating.

When all the beef, vegetables and fruit have been eaten, add the bean sprouts to the fondue pot and heat through for 1–2 minutes. Ladle into soup bowls and drink to clear the palate.

LAMB *in* SPICY YOGURT SAUCE

HEAT 3–4

Serves 4

2 tbsp sunflower or olive oil

4 lean boneless lamb steaks, about
150 g/5 oz each

1 onion, sliced

2 garlic cloves, crushed

3 green New Mexico chillies, peeled,
deseeded and sliced

1 tsp ground cumin

½ tsp ground cloves

1 tsp ground cinnamon

12 green cardamom pods

200 ml/7 fl oz water

300 ml/½ pt natural yogurt

25 g/1 oz ground almonds

25 g/1 oz toasted flaked almonds

flat-leaf parsley, to garnish

Heat the oil in a frying pan and seal the lamb on both sides. Drain on paper towels and reserve.

Add the onion, garlic and chillies to the pan and sauté for 5 minutes, or until soft. Stir in the spices and cook for a further 3 minutes. Add the water to the pan and bring to the boil. Reduce the heat and add the lamb, then simmer for 10 minutes.

Stir the yogurt and ground almonds into the pan and cook for a further 15 minutes, or until the lamb is tender. Stir frequently during this time. (If the sauce is thickening too much, add a little extra water.)

Sprinkle the lamb and sauce with the flaked almonds and garnish with parsley.

LAMB TIKKA

HEAT 7–8

Serves 4

450 g/1 lb lean boneless lamb,
trimmed

150 ml/¼ pt natural yogurt

2 tbsp tandoori paste

1 tsp ground coriander

1 tsp ground cumin

1 tsp turmeric

1 tsp ground ginger

3 garlic cloves, crushed

grated rind of 1 lemon

6 green serrano chillies, deseeded and
finely chopped

2 tbsp freshly chopped mint

8 baby onions

2 courgettes, trimmed and cut into
4 cm/1½ in chunks

2 red peppers, deseeded and
cut into wedges

lemon wedges, to garnish

The correct way to cook a tikka dish is in a tandoori oven but as these are not readily available, grilling or barbecuing works just as well. The longer the meat is marinated, the better the flavour.

Cut the lamb into 4 cm/1½ in cubes and place in a shallow dish. Put the yogurt into a bowl and mix in the tandoori paste, spices, garlic, lemon rind, chillies and 1 tbsp of the mint. Spoon the marinade over the lamb, cover and chill for at least 4 hours, turning occasionally.

Preheat the grill to moderately hot just before cooking.

Thread the lamb alternately with the prepared vegetables on to kebab skewers and cook under the grill for 10–15 minutes, or until cooked as preferred. Brush with the marinade during cooking. Serve sprinkled with the remaining chopped mint and lemon wedges.

KASHMIR LAMB

Serves 4

3 tbsp sunflower oil or ghee

1 large onion, sliced

2 garlic cloves

2–3 New Mexico red chillies,
deseeded and sliced

2.5 cm/1 in piece root ginger, peeled
and grated

1 tsp ground cumin

1 tsp turmeric

1 tsp ratan jot or few drops of
red food colouring

450 g/1 lb lamb fillet, trimmed
and cubed

4 tomatoes, peeled, deseeded and
chopped

450 ml/¾ pt lamb or vegetable stock

25 g/1 oz pistachio nuts

50 g/2 oz cashew nuts

25 g/1 oz sultanas

1 tbsp freshly chopped coriander

freshly cooked rice, to serve

Kashmir dishes are usually red in colour and this is achieved by the use of ratan jot, a red herb food colouring. Kashmir foods are normally very rich and creamy due to the use of the nuts grown in the area.

Heat the oil or ghee in a large pan and sauté the onion, garlic, chillies and ginger for 5 minutes. Add the spices and sauté for a further 3 minutes, then stir in the ratan jot or food colouring. Add the lamb in two batches and cook for 5 minutes, or until sealed, stirring frequently.

Add the tomatoes and stock, and bring to the boil. Cover with a lid, reduce the heat and simmer for 40 minutes, stirring occasionally.

Add the nuts and sultanas, and simmer for a further 15 minutes, or until the meat is tender. Stir in the coriander and serve with freshly cooked rice.

PORK *and* CHILLI BALLS

HEAT 6

Serves 4

450 g/1 lb lean ground pork

3 lemon grass stalks, outer leaves
    discarded and minced

1 tbsp Red Chilli Paste (page 47)

zested rind of 1 lime

3 tomatoes, peeled, deseeded and
    finely chopped

1 tsp turmeric

2 tsp minced galangal, or peeled and
    minced root ginger

1 garlic clove, minced

¼ tsp salt

oil for deep-frying

lime wedges and chilli flowers
    (page 11), to garnish

❧ Put the pork, lemon grass, Red Chilli Paste and lime zest into a bowl. Stir in the tomatoes, turmeric, galangal or ginger, garlic and salt. Mix together well.

❧ Using slightly wet hands, form the pork mixture into small balls about the size of an apricot. Chill, covered, for at least 30 minutes.

❧ Heat the oil to 180°C/350°F and fry the balls in batches for 5–6 minutes, or until golden. Drain on paper towels. Serve garnished with lime wedges and chilli flowers.

HOT *and* SPICY
BARBECUED SPARE RIBS

HEAT 6

Serves 4

675 g/1½ lb Chinese spare ribs

Marinade

4 Hontaka or Thai red chillies,
    deseeded and chopped

300 ml/½ pt chicken stock

juice of 2 limes

1 tbsp soy sauce

1 tbsp hoisin sauce

1 tbsp muscovado sugar

2 tbsp tomato purée

2 tsp Worcestershire sauce

1 tsp ground cinnamon

½ tsp ground cloves

6 spring onions, trimmed and chopped

A nice, thoughtful gesture is to provide some finger bowls filled with warm water and a slice of lemon and some paper towels so that diners can rinse their fingers after eating this dish.

❧ Cut the spare ribs into separate ribs if necessary and place in a shallow dish. Mix all the marinade ingredients, except the spring onions, together in a pan and bring to the boil. Simmer for 2 minutes, allow to cool and then add the spring onions.

❧ Pour the marinade over the ribs, turning them to ensure they are well covered. Cover the dish and leave in the refrigerator to marinate for at least 4 hours, turning occasionally and spooning the marinade over.

❧ Preheat the oven to 190°C/375°F/Gas Mark 5.

❧ Drain the ribs and place on a rack in a roasting tin with a little water in the base. Brush the ribs with the marinade and turn occasionally during cooking. Cook for 1–1¼ hours, basting occasionally.

Pork and Chilli Balls ▶

Serves 4

3 red poblano chillies

1 garlic clove

4 tbsp olive or sunflower oil

2 tbsp orange juice

2 tsp clear honey, warmed

4 gammon or ham steaks, trimmed
  of excess fat

25 g/1 oz butter

150 ml/¼pt dry white wine

150 ml/¼ pt chicken or
  vegetable stock

7.5 cm/3 in piece of cucumber, thinly
  peeled and cut into julienne strips

1 tbsp cornflour

1 tbsp water

orange wedges and fresh herbs
  to garnish

BRAISED HAM *with* CHILLI SAUCE

Preheat the grill.

Place the chillies in a grill pan and cook for about 10 minutes, or until the skins have blistered and charred. Put into a polythene bag for 10 minutes before peeling and discarding the seeds.

Put the chillies into a food processor with the garlic, oil, orange juice and honey. Blend until smooth, then use to brush over both sides of the gammon or ham steaks. Leave in a cool place for at least 30 minutes.

Melt the butter in a large frying pan and seal the steaks quickly on both sides. Add any remaining chilli marinade, the wine and stock. Bring to the boil, then reduce the heat and simmer for 5–8 minutes, or until the steaks are cooked. Drain and place on warmed serving plates.

Add the cucumber to the pan, together with the cornflour blended with the water. Cook, stirring occasionally, for 2 minutes, or until the sauce has thickened. Pour over the steaks and garnish with orange wedges and fresh herbs.

CHILLI BEEF-BURGER

Serves 4

50 g/2 oz fresh white bread, crusts
   removed

4 tbsp milk

675 g/1½ lb rump or chuck steak,
   trimmed and minced

6 spring onions, trimmed and
   finely chopped

4 red Anaheim chillies, deseeded and
   finely chopped

1 tbsp freshly chopped oregano

salt and pepper

2 tbsp sunflower oil

2 onions, sliced

4 hamburger baps

Chilli Mayonnaise (page 44)

½ small iceburg lettuce, shredded

2 large tomatoes, sliced

Chilli Pepper Relish (page 47)

🌶 Soak the bread in the milk for 10 minutes, then drain and press out any excess liquid. Reserve.

🌶 Combine the beef with the soaked bread, spring onions, 3 of the chillies, and the oregano with seasoning to taste. Mix together well. Slightly wet your hands and shape the mixture into four large burgers.

🌶 Heat the oil in a frying pan and gently sauté the onions and remaining chilli for 5–8 minutes until softened. Drain on paper towels and keep warm.

🌶 Preheat the grill to moderately hot. Grill the burgers for 10 minutes, or until cooked to personal preference, turning at least once during cooking.

🌶 Split the baps and lightly toast. Spread the bases with the Chilli Mayonnaise and arrange some shredded lettuce on top. Place the cooked burgers on the lettuce and top with the cooked onions and chillies, sliced tomatoes and Chilli Pepper Relish. Replace the bap tops and serve immediately.

BEEF RENDANG

Serves 4

4 chipotle dried chillies, roasted,
   rehydrated (page 16) and chopped

2 shallots, chopped

1 garlic clove, crushed

2 tbsp sunflower oil

675 g/1½ lb braising steak, trimmed
   and cubed

1 tsp turmeric

600 ml/1 pt coconut milk

2 kaffir lime leaves

juice of 2 limes

salt and pepper

50 g/2 oz creamed coconut

freshly cooked rice, to serve

The dried chillies can be replaced with 3–4 red fresno chillies or 1–2 Thai (bird's eye) chillies. If a thickened sauce is preferred, add 1–1½ tbsp of flour when adding the turmeric. Check during cooking that the sauce is not becoming too thick; if it is, add a little more coconut milk or stock.

🌶 Make a paste with the chillies, shallots and garlic, and reserve.

🌶 Heat the oil in a large pan and sauté the beef in batches for 5 minutes, or until sealed. Remove from the pan with a slotted spoon and reserve.

🌶 Add the paste to the oil remaining in the pan and gently fry for 5 minutes. Add the beef and turmeric to the pan and cook for 2 minutes, stirring constantly.

🌶 Pour in the coconut milk and add the lime leaves, juice and seasoning. Bring to the boil, cover the pan and reduce the heat. Simmer for 1½ hours, or until the meat is tender.

🌶 Add the creamed coconut gradually to the pan, stirring after each addition. Heat through for 5 minutes and serve with freshly cooked rice.

HEAT 8

Serves 4

300 ml 1½ pt red wine

1 tbsp Worcestershire sauce

5 tbsp sunflower oil

4 red Scotch bonnet chillies, deseeded and sliced

1 tbsp roughly chopped fresh oregano

225 g/8 oz rump steak, trimmed and cut into thin strips

1 red onion, cut into thin wedges

1 small red pepper, deseeded and cut into thin strips

1 small yellow pepper, deseeded and cut into thin strips

1 courgette, trimmed and cut into thin strips

8–12 wheat tortillas, lightly warmed, soured cream, Salsa Verde (page 47) and Guacamole (page 29), to serve

BEEF FAJITAS

Fajitas are generally made from a poorer quality cut of beef that has been marinated and then sliced across the grain and barbecued over a fierce heat. They should be served immediately which is why many restaurants call this dish sizzling beef. For this recipe a better quality of beef has been used but if you prefer, substitute skirt or chuck beef.

Mix the wine, Worcestershire sauce, 3 tbsp of the oil, 2 of the chillies and oregano together. Put the beef into a shallow dish and pour over the wine marinade. Cover and leave for at least 1 hour. Drain, reserving a little of the marinade.

Heat the remaining oil in a wok or large pan and quickly fry the remaining chillies and the vegetables for 3–5 minutes, or until crisp and slightly blackened on the edges. Remove from the pan and reserve.

Fry the beef in batches in the oil remaining in the pan for 2–3 minutes or until sealed and browned and drain on paper towels. When all the meat has been browned, return the vegetables and 3–4 tbsp of the reserved marinade to the pan and heat through over a fierce heat, stirring frequently.

To serve, spread each warmed tortilla with soured cream, then place some of the beef mixture on top and add a spoonful of Salsa Verde. Roll up and eat with extra Salsa Verde and Guacamole.

HEAT 8–10

Serves 4

2 tbsp sunflower or groundnut oil

2.5 cm/1 in. piece root ginger, peeled and grated

2–3 hontaka or Thai red chillies, deseeded and chopped

350 g/12 oz pork fillet, trimmed and cut into thin strips

1 red pepper, deseeded and cut into strips

1 yellow pepper, deseeded and cut into strips

6 spring onions, trimmed and sliced diagonally

1 tbsp tomato purée

1 tbsp water

2 tsp soy sauce

1 tsp clear honey

1 tsp sesame oil

spring onion tassel and flat-leaf parsley, to garnish

SICHUAN HOT CHILLI PORK

Sichuan cuisine is becoming increasingly popular in the west and there are many different variations on any Sichuan dish. Some err on the sweet side, but nearly all have a strong chilli slant.

Heat the oil in a wok or large pan and stir-fry the ginger and chillies for 2 minutes. Add the pork and stir-fry for a further 4–5 minutes. Then add the peppers and cook for 2 minutes.

Add the spring onions and stir-fry for 30 seconds. Then add the tomato purée blended with the water, the soy sauce and honey. Stir-fry for 1 minute, add the sesame oil and give one more stir. Serve immediately garnished with a spring onion tassel and flat-leaf parsley.

Beef Fajitas ▶

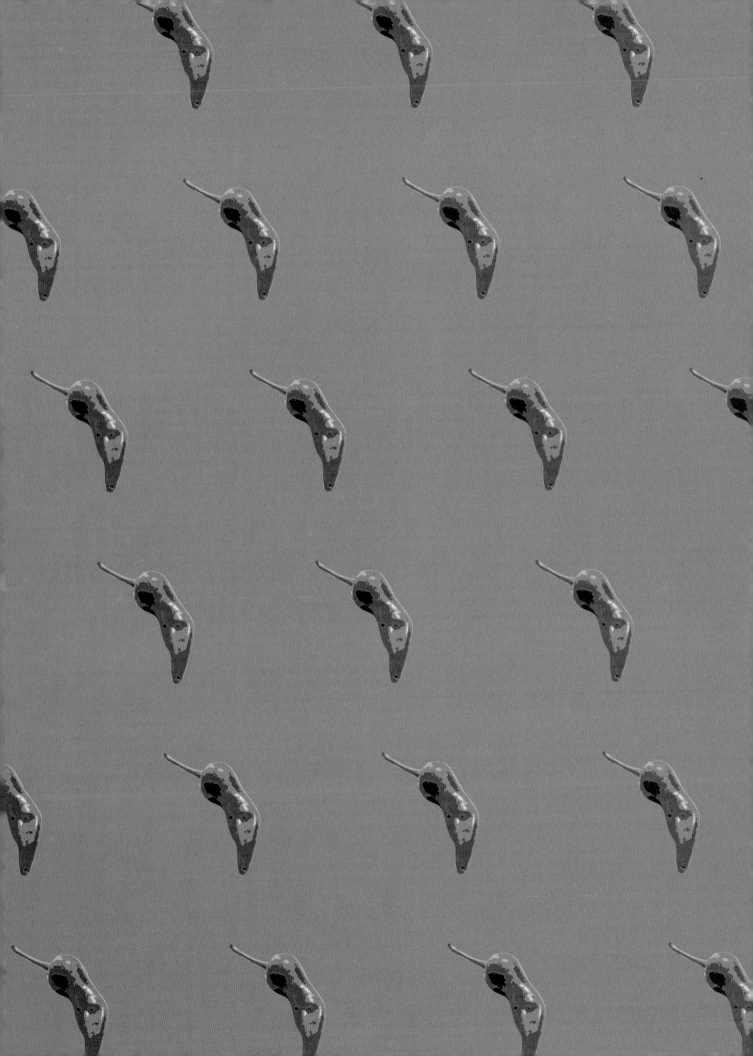

Chapter 8

Vegetarian

Serves 4

8 prepared wheat tortillas

Sauce
2 tsp sunflower oil
1 small onion, chopped
2 red jalapeño chillies, deseeded and
*   chopped*
400 g/14 oz can chopped tomatoes

Filling
½ small iceburg lettuce, shredded
225 g/8 oz Frijoles Refritos (page 28)
50 g/2 oz hard cheese, such as
*   Cheddar, grated*
4 spring onions, trimmed and chopped
2 red jalapeño chillies, deseeded and
*   chopped*
soured cream and lime wedges,
*   to serve*

Serves 5

1 tbsp sunflower oil
2 onions, sliced
2 garlic cloves, crushed
4 rocotillo chillies, deseeded
*   and chopped*
1 tsp turmeric
175 g/6 oz green lentils
600 ml/1 pint water
salt and pepper
1 red pepper, deseeded, chopped
*   and blanched*
lightly fried onions and freshly
*   chopped parsley, to garnish*

CHALUPAS

Tortillas

Tortillas are the bases for many Mexican dishes such as enchilidas, burritos and empanadas. They are often filled with a variety of savoury mixtures and almost always served with a side dish of refried beans. Here they are served crisp as filled tacos shells.

🌶 Heat the oil in a small pan and gently sauté the onion and chillies for 5 minutes. Stir in the chopped tomatoes and bring to the boil. Reduce the heat and simmer for 15 minutes. Allow to cool slightly, then pass through a sieve to form a smooth purée. Cover and keep warm.

🌶 Warm the tortillas slightly by placing in a non-stick frying pan for about 30 seconds. Dampen the edges, then shape and pinch up the sides to form a boat shape.

🌶 Fill the tortillas with the shredded lettuce and place the Frijoles Refritos on top. Spoon a little of the prepared sauce over. Divide the cheese between the tortillas and sprinkle over with the scallions and chopped chillies. Serve with soured cream and lime wedges.

CHILLI PEPPER DAL

Dal, or dhal, is a traditional Indian side dish or snack, and can be made from green or red lentils with assorted seasonings. Sometimes the mixture is formed into rissoles when served.

🌶 Heat the oil and sauté the onion, garlic and chillies for 5 minutes. Stir in the turmeric and sauté for a further minute.

🌶 Rinse and pick over the lentils if necessary; then add to the pan with the water and seasoning to taste. Bring to the boil. Cover the pan, then reduce the heat and simmer for 35 minutes, or until cooked. (You may need to add a little extra water if the mixture is becoming too dry.)

🌶 Stir the chopped, blanched red pepper into the dal for the last 10 minutes of cooking time. Adjust the seasoning and serve sprinkled with fried onions and parsley.

Chalupas ▶

HEAT 5

Serves 4

2 tbsp olive oil

1 large onion, chopped

1 small fennel bulb, trimmed
    and chopped

2 garlic cloves, crushed

4 red de agua chillies, deseeded
    and sliced

8 sun-dried tomatoes

450-600 ml/¾-1 pt vegetable stock

225 g/8 oz carrot, grated

100 g/4 oz oyster mushrooms, wiped
    and sliced

2 tbsp tomato purée

1 tsp sugar

salt and pepper

2 red peppers, deseeded, blanched
    and cut into small strips

2 tbsp freshly chopped basil

300-350 g/10-12 oz fresh pasta,
    such as tagliatelle or rigatoni

shaved or freshly grated Parmesan
    cheese, to serve

freshly chopped basil, to garnish

PASTA *with* SPICY TOMATO SAUCE

Heat the oil in a pan and gently sauté the onion, fennel, garlic, chillies and sun-dried tomatoes for 3 minutes. Add 150 ml/¼ pt of the stock and simmer for 5–8 minutes.

Put into a food processor and blend to a chunky purée, adding extra stock if necessary. Return to the pan with all but 4 tbsp of the remaining stock.

Add the carrot, mushrooms, the tomato purée blended with the remaining stock, sugar and seasoning to taste. Bring to the boil and simmer gently for 15–20 minutes, or until a thick consistency is formed. Add the peppers and chopped basil, and cook for a further 3–4 minutes.

Meanwhile, cook the pasta in boiling salted water for 4–6 minutes, or until al dente. Drain and return to the pan. Pour over the tomato sauce and toss well. Heat through for 2–3 minutes, stirring frequently. Garnish with freshly chopped basil and served sprinkled with Parmesan.

SPICY VEGETABLE TACOS

HEAT 5

Serves 4

8 ready-made taco shells

1 tbsp sunflower oil

1 onion, thickly sliced

4 red de agua chillies, deseeded
    and sliced

1 orange pepper, deseeded and cut
    into thick strips

1 large courgette, trimmed and cut
    into strips

200 g/7 oz canned pinto beans,
    drained and rinsed

200 g/7 oz can chopped tomatoes

½ small iceberg lettuce, shredded

2 ripe avocados, peeled, sliced and
    tossed in 3 tbsp lemon juice

175 g/6 oz Cheddar cheese, grated
    Chilli Mayonnaise (page 44), 6 tbsp

soured cream and canned chillies,
    to serve

Traditionally, a taco is a hand-held tortilla folded over the filling. The tortilla is warmed first so it folds easily. Now it is more usual to buy the ready-made taco shells. But don't forget to warm them first.

Preheat the oven to 180°C/350°F/Gas Mark 4. Place the taco shells, open end down, on a baking sheet and heat for 2-3 minutes. Reserve.

Heat the oil in a pan and sauté the onion and chillies for 5 minutes. Add the orange pepper and courgette, and cook for a further 3 minutes. Add the beans and tomatoes, and cook for 8 minutes, stirring frequently, or until a thick consistency is reached.

Fill the heated taco shells with the shredded lettuce and top with the chilli and bean mixture. Place the sliced avocados on top and sprinkle with the grated cheese. Serve immediately with the Chilli Mayonnaise, the soured cream and canned chillies.

Pasta with Spicy Tomato sauce ▶

FRIED THAI NOODLES
with CHILLIES *and* VEGETABLES

Serves 4

175 g/6 oz instant dried noodles

2 tbsp sunflower oil

2 lemon grass stalks, outer leaves
   removed and chopped

2.5 cm/1 in piece root ginger, peeled
   and grated

1 red onion, cut into thin wedges

2 garlic cloves, crushed

4 red Thai chillies, deseeded and sliced

1 red pepper, deseeded and cut into
   matchsticks

100 g/4 oz carrot, very thinly sliced
   with a vegetable peeler

100 g/4 oz courgettes, trimmed and
   sliced with a vegetable peeler

75 g/3 oz mangetout, trimmed and
   cut diagonally in half

6 spring onions, trimmed and
   diagonally sliced

100 g/4 oz cashew nuts

2 tbsp soy sauce

juice of 1 orange

1 tsp clear honey

1 tbsp sesame oil

Rice or noodles, whether boiled or fried, form the basis of most meals in Thailand. Thai cooking is often pungent and hot but at the same time is slightly perfumed. This is often due to the lemon grass which features strongly in most of their dishes.

⟋ Cook the noodles in lightly salted boiling water for 3 minutes. Drain, plunge into cold water, then drain again and reserve.

⟋ Heat the oil in a wok or large pan and stir-fry the lemon grass and ginger for 2 minutes. Discard the lemon grass and ginger, keeping the oil in the pan.

⟋ Add the onion, garlic and chillies, and stir-fry for 2 minutes. Add the red pepper and cook for a further 2 minutes. Add the remaining vegetables and stir-fry for 2 minutes. Then add the reserved noodles and cashew nuts with the soy sauce, orange juice and honey. Stir-fry for 1 minute. Add the sesame oil and stir-fry for 30 seconds. Serve immediately.

OKRA *and* BEAN CURRY

Serves 4

2 tbsp sunflower oil

1 large onion, sliced

2 garlic cloves, crushed

4 Kenyan or green fresno chillies,
   deseeded and sliced

1 tsp ground coriander

1 tsp ground cumin

5 cloves, ground

8 green cardamom pods

1 tsp turmeric

1 tsp fenugreek seeds, lightly bruised

450 ml/¾ pt vegetable stock

450 g/1 lb okra, trimmed

400 g/14 oz can pinto or kidney
   beans, drained and rinsed

4 tbsp natural yogurt

2 tbsp freshly chopped coriander

25 g/1 oz toasted flaked almonds

⟋ Heat the oil in a pan and sauté the onion, garlic and chillies for 5 minutes. Add the spices and sauté for a further 3 minutes. Stir in the stock and bring to the boil. Cover the pan, reduce the heat and simmer for 10 minutes.

⟋ Prick the okra a few times with a fork and add to the pan with the beans. Cook gently for 8–10 minutes, or until the okra is tender. Stir in the yogurt and coriander, and heat through for a further minute. Serve sprinkled with the almonds.

◀ Fried Thai Noodles with
   Chillies and Vegetables

Serves 4

8 red poblano or red New
   Mexico chillies
25 g/1 oz butter
225 g/8 oz ripe tomatoes, peeled,
   deseeded and sliced
juice of 2 limes
2 firm, almost ripe avocados, peeled
   and stones removed
salad leaves, to serve

Sauce
50 g/2 oz pecan or walnuts
25 g/1 oz blanched almonds
150 ml/¼ pt crème fraîche
1 tsp clear honey
2 tbsp Parmesan cheese, grated

CHILLIES *in* NUT SAUCE

Chillis en nogado

Traditionally, this dish is green, white and red, the colours of the Mexican flag. Ideally green walnuts are used for the sauce but if these are unavailable, ripe walnuts can be substituted.

❧ Finely grind the nuts for the sauce in a food processor. Combine with the crème fraîche and honey. Put into a small saucepan and stir in the cheese. Heat through gently, stirring frequently.
❧ Preheat the grill.
❧ Place the chillies in a grill pan and cook for 10 minutes until the skins have blistered and started to blacken. Remove from the heat and put into a polythene bag. Leave for 10 minutes. Skin the chillies and discard the seeds and membrane. Cut into strips.
❧ Melt the butter in a pan and sauté the chillies for 5 minutes. Add the chopped tomatoes and lime juice, and sauté for a further 3 minutes. Slice the avocados, add to the pan and heat through for 5 minutes stirring occasionally.
❧ Serve on a bed of salad leaves with the nut sauce.

Serves 4

2 tbsp sunflower oil
1 large onion, thinly sliced
2 garlic cloves, crushed
4 green de agua chillies, deseeded
   and sliced
350 g/12 oz ripe tomatoes, peeled,
   deseeded and chopped
1 tbsp tomato purée
1 tbsp water
2 courgettes, trimmed and cut
   into matchsticks
175 g/6 oz cheese, such as Cheshire
   or Lancashire, grated
6 spring onions, trimmed and chopped
8 wheat tortillas
fresh herbs, to garnish
Pepper Relish (page 47), to serve

VEGETARIAN ENCHILADAS

Most people associate Mexican food with snacks such as tacos or enchiladas, which the Mexicans call antojitos, meaning little whim or craving. They nearly all consist of a tortilla presented in a variety of ways and can be found at roadside cafés, market places and stalls to be eaten at any time of the day.

❧ Preheat the oven to 200°C/400°F/Gas Mark 6.
❧ Heat the oil in a frying pan and gently sauté the onion, garlic and chillies for 5 minutes. Add the tomatoes and the tomato purée blended with the water and bring to the boil. Cover the pan, reduce the heat and simmer for 15 minutes. Add the courgettes, 100 g/4 oz of the cheese and the spring onions, and stir well.
❧ Divide the filling between the tortillas and fold into quarters. Place in a shallow ovenproof dish and sprinkle with the remaining cheese. Bake for 15 minutes, or until the cheese is bubbly. Garnish with herbs and serve immediately with Pepper Relish.

Vegetarian Enchiladas ▶

HEAT 5

Serves 4

450 g/1 lb okra

2 tbsp sunflower oil

1 large onion, thinly sliced

4 green Anaheim chillies, deseeded
   and sliced

1 green pepper, deseeded and sliced

175 g/6 oz tomatoes, peeled,
   deseeded and chopped

salt and pepper

3 tbsp water

natural yogurt, to serve

BRAISED OKRA
with CHILLIES

Trim the okra and prick a few times with a fork.

Heat the oil in a pan and sauté the onion and chillies for 5 minutes, or until softened. Add the green pepper and cook for a further 2 minutes.

Stir in the chopped tomatoes, the okra and water with seasoning to taste and bring to the boil. Reduce the heat, cover the pan and simmer for 8 minutes, or until the okra is tender. Serve immediately topped with spoonfuls of yogurt.

Braised Okra with Chillies and above, ▶
Potatoes with Chilli, Peanuts and Cheese

SPICY PEPPER PIZZA

Serves 4

1 tbsp sunflower oil

1 onion, chopped

2 garlic cloves, crushed

5 red jalapeño chillies, deseeded
  and thinly sliced

400 g/14 oz can chopped tomatoes

2 tbsp tomato purée

2 tbsp freshly chopped oregano

2 tsp ground cumin

2 prepared 20 cm/8 in pizza bases

2 red peppers, skinned and deseeded

2 green peppers, skinned and
  deseeded

2 yellow peppers, skinned and
  deseeded

175 g/6 oz mozzarella cheese, grated

50 g/2 oz pitted black olives

Preheat the oven to 200°C/400°F Gas Mark 6. Lightly oil two baking sheets.

Heat the oil in a pan and sauté the onion, garlic and chillies for 5 minutes. Add the chopped tomatoes, tomato purée, oregano and cumin, and bring to the boil. Reduce the heat and simmer for 10–15 minutes, or until a thick sauce consistency is reached.

Spread the sauce over the pizza bases. Slice the peppers and arrange on top of the sauce. Cover with the cheese and arrange the olives on top. Bake for 25 minutes, or until the cheese is golden and bubbly.

HEAT 4–5

Serves 4

Sauce

225 g/8 oz green tomatoes, peeled,
    deseeded and chopped

3 shallots, finely chopped

2–3 garlic cloves, crushed

3 green jalapeño chillies, deseeded
    and chopped

150 ml/¼ pt vegetable stock

1 tsp clear honey

2 tsp arrowroot

1 tbsp water

sliced green chilli to garnish

Turnovers

225 g/8 oz Cheddar cheese, grated

6 spring onions, trimmed and chopped

50 g/2 oz pine kernels, toasted

6 dried chipotle chillies, roasted and
    rehydrated (page 16)

25 g/1 oz butter

225 g/8 oz mushrooms, wiped
    and sliced

8 prepared wheat tortillas

1 (size 5) egg, beaten

oil for deep-frying

salad leaves, to serve

CHEESE TURNOVERS
with GREEN TOMATO SAUCE

Enchiladas with Salsa Verde

Enchiladas were first made by the American Indians. In the northern state of Sonora they developed a white flour tortilla after the Spanish had introduced wheat to the region. These are usually larger than corn tortillas and they too are often used for making burritos.

➊ Make the sauce. Put the green tomatoes, shallots, garlic and chillies into a saucepan and simmer for 5-7 minutes, or until softened. Then put into a food processor with the stock and honey and blend to a purée. Pass through a sieve.

➋ Return to the pan and simmer for 5 minutes. Blend the arrowroot with the water and stir into the sauce. Cook, stirring constantly until the sauce thickens and clears. If not to be used immediately, thicken when required and store, covered, in the refrigerator.

➌ Mix the cheese, spring onions and pine kernels together. Discard the seeds from the rehydrated chillies and chop. Add to the cheese mixture and mix together well. Reserve.

➍ Melt the butter in a small pan and sauté the mushrooms for 3 minutes. Drain.

➎ Place a spoonful of the cheese mixture on top of each tortilla and top with a spoonful of the mushrooms. Brush the edges of each tortilla with a little beaten egg, then fold over to form a pasty shape and pinch the edges together firmly. Brush the edges lightly with the beaten egg and fold the edges over again to give a rope effect and a more secure seal.

➏ Heat the oil to 180°C/350°F and fry the turnovers in batches for 2–3 minutes, or until golden. Drain on paper towels and serve on a bed of salad leaves, and the green sauce.

HEAT 2–3

Serves 4

8 fresh banana or other large chillies
    about 15 cm/6 in in length

1 tsp chilli powder

225 g/8 oz prepared Frijoles
    Refritos (page 28)

3 tbsp plain flour

3 (size 3) eggs, separated

oil for deep-frying

1 fresh red Anaheim chilli, deseeded
    and sliced

2 tbsp freshly chopped
    flat-leaf parsley

zested lime rind

Salsa Verde (page 47) to serve

STUFFED CHILLIES *with* BEANS

Chilli rellenos de frijoles

➊ Preheat the grill to high. Place the chillies in a grill pan and cook until the skins blister and begin to blacken. Remove from the heat and put into a polythene bag. Leave for about 10 minute to allow the chillies to sweat, then carefully discard the skins. Make a slit down the centre lengthways and discard the seeds and membrane. Sprinkle with chilli powder.

➋ Stuff the chillies with the Frijoles Refritos and overlap the edges to encase the filling.

➌ Sift a scant 2 tbsp of the flour into a bowl, then add the egg yolks and beat well to form a smooth consistency. Whisk the egg whites until stiff and standing in peaks, then carefully fold into the egg yolk mixture.

➍ Pour the oil into a pan to a depth of about 5 cm/2 in and heat to 180°C/350°F.

➎ Coat the stuffed chillies in the remaining flour and dip into the batter. Fry in the hot oil for 3–4 minutes, or until golden brown. Drain on paper towels, then arrange on a serving plate and sprinkle with the sliced chillies, herbs and lime zest. Serve with Salsa Verde.

Enchiladas with Salsa Verde ▶

CAULIFLOWER and TOMATO CURRY

Gobbi tamatar

HEAT 5

Serves 4

450 g/1 lb cauliflower florets

225 g/8 oz potatoes, diced

2 tbsp sunflower oil

5 cm/2 in. piece root ginger, peeled
  and grated

1 onion, sliced

2 garlic cloves, crushed

5 dried ancho chillies, roasted and
  rehydrated (page 16)

1 tsp coriander seeds

1 tsp cumin seeds

1 tsp fenugreek seeds

1 tsp turmeric

2 tbsp tomato purée

2 tbsp water

450 g/1 lb tomatoes, peeled,
  deseeded and chopped

150 ml/¼ pt coconut milk

150 ml/¼ pt natural yogurt

fresh flat-leaf parsley or coriander,
  to garnish

naan bread, freshly cooked rice,
poppadoms and chutneys, to serve

If dried chillies are unavailable, use 3–4 green fresno chillies or 1–1½ tsp medium-hot chilli powder.

🌶 Cook the cauliflower in lightly salted boiling water for 3 minutes, drain and reserve

🌶 Cook the potatoes in lightly salted boiling water for 10 minutes, or until just tender. Drain and reserve.

🌶 Heat the oil in a large pan and gently sauté the ginger for 3 minutes. Then discard the ginger. Add the onion, garlic and chopped rehydrated chillies, and sauté for 3 minutes. Add the spices and cook, stirring frequently, for 3 minutes.

🌶 Blend the tomato purée with the water and add to the pan with the tomatoes and coconut milk. Bring to just below boiling point and simmer for 5 minutes. Add the reserved cauliflower and potatoes, and cook for a further 5–8 minutes, or until cooked.

🌶 Stir in the yogurt and heat through for 2 minutes. Garnish with fresh herbs and serve with warm naan bread and rice, poppadoms and chutneys.

SAG ALOO SAMOSAS

HEAT 3–4

Serves 4

3 tbsp sunflower oil

1 onion, chopped

3 green fresno chillies, deseeded
   and chopped

1 tsp ground cumin

1 tsp ground coriander

100 g/4 oz potatoes,
   cooked and diced

100 g/4 oz carrots, cooked and diced

350 g/12 oz spinach, cooked
   and chopped

4 large sheets filo pastry

oil for deep-frying

green salad, naan and assorted
   chutneys, to serve

Samosas are a typical Indian snack with every region having its own particular filling. It takes a little practice to achieve a good shape, but once you have mastered the art you will be surprised how easy they are in fact to prepare.

Heat the sunflower oil in a pan and sauté the onion and chillies for 3 minutes. Add the spices and sauté for a further 3 minutes. Then add the cooked vegetables and mix well together. Allow to cool.

Cut the filo pastry into 25 x 10 cm/10 x 4 in strips. Place 2 tbsp of the filling at one end of each strip and fold the pastry over diagonally to form a triangle. Continue folding triangles along the strip, brushing the edges with a little water.

Heat the oil for deep frying to 180°C/350°F and fry the samosas in batches for about 5 minutes, or until golden. Drain on paper towels and serve with green salad, naan and assorted chutneys.

ACAR ACAR

Indonesian mixed vegetables

HEAT 8

Serves 4

4 Thai red chillies

1 large onion, chopped

3 garlic cloves

225 g/8 oz fresh peanuts, shelled
   and roasted

3 tbsp sunflower oil

40 g/1½ oz granulated sugar

600 ml/1 pt white wine vinegar

225 g/8 oz green beans

1 cucumber

2 red peppers, deseeded

225 g/8 oz cauliflower florets

1 fresh pineapple, flesh removed
   from shell, cored and diced

salt and pepper

a few threads of saffron or
   ½ tsp turmeric

A Malaysian pickle similar to piccalilli. Often served with curries or cold meat or even fish dishes.

Put the chillies, onion and garlic into a food processor and blend until smooth. Reserve. Grind or process the peanuts until lightly chopped and reserve.

Heat the oil in a large pan and gently sauté the chilli purée for 4 minutes. Add the sugar and vinegar, bring to the boil and simmer for 5 minutes.

Add the peanut paste and then the vegetables and pineapple with the seasoning and saffron or turmeric. Simmer for 2 minutes, stirring constantly. If serving hot, heat through gently for 4–5 minutes, stirring frequently. If serving cold, heat through for 2 minutes, then place in a serving dish, cover and chill. Stir thoroughly before serving.

If stored in sealed screw-topped glass jars, Acar Acar may be kept in the refrigerator or a cool place for up to 1 month.

SPICED AUBERGINE PURÉE

Serves 6

2 large aubergines, about 450 g/1 lb
 in weight

4 red Anaheim chillies

4 garlic cloves

grated rind and juice of 1 large lemon

1 tsp ground cumin

1 tsp ground coriander

1 tsp ground cinnamon

175 g/6 oz soft cream cheese

cumin seeds to garnish

pitta breads and crudités, to serve

Preheat the oven to 200°C/400°F/Gas Mark 6.

Rinse the aubergines and prick a few times. Place in the oven directly on an oven shelf and bake for 40 minutes, or until very soft and the aubergines have begun to collapse. Place the chillies and garlic on a baking sheet and place on another shelf. Cook the chillies and garlic for about 10 minutes, or until the skins have begun to wrinkle. Remove from the oven and put into a polythene bag for 10 minutes. Peel and discard the seeds from the chillies and the skins from the garlic, and reserve.

Allow the aubergines to cool, then strip off the skin and put the flesh into a food processor with the chillies, garlic, lemon rind and juice, and the spices. Blend to form a smooth purée, then add the cream cheese and blend again. Transfer to a serving bowl and fork the top.

Chill for at least 30 minutes. Garnish with cumin seeds and serve with pitta breads and crudités.

INDEX